Central Park's Adventure-Style Playgrounds

CENTRAL PARK'S ADVENTURE-STYLE PLAYGROUNDS

Renewal of a Midcentury Legacy

Marie Warsh

WITH A FOREWORD BY
M. Paul Friedberg

An initiative of The Cultural Landscape Foundation
Charles A. Birnbaum, Series Editor

Published by Louisiana State University Press  Baton Rouge

Modern Landscapes

TRANSITION & TRANSFORMATION

This Cultural Landscape Foundation series focuses on historically important midcentury works that have undergone significant change. Each publication in the series chronicles the planning and design motivations behind the work, illuminates its history, places it within its historical design context, and, perhaps most importantly, draws attention to midcentury landscape treasures while raising awareness of their unique design value, inherent vulnerability, and historic preservation needs. Edited by Charles A. Birnbaum, the foundation's president, the series balances programmatic, design, historic preservation, and environmental concerns while providing a best-practices model. Depending on the landscape, this may include research and documentation efforts, design and treatment interventions, or ongoing management practices and strategies.

ALSO IN THIS SERIES:

Mellon Square, by Susan M. Rademacher
Lawrence Halprin's Skyline Park, by Ann Komara

This project has been made possible in part by the New York State Council on the Arts with the support of Governor Andrew Cuomo and the New York State Legislature.

Published by Louisiana State University Press

Manufactured in the United States of America
First printing

Designer: Michelle A. Neustrom
Typeface: Helvetica Now
Printer and binder: Sheridan Books, Inc.

Cataloging-in-Publication Data are available at the Library of Congress.

ISBN 978-0-8071-7201-8 (pbk: alk. paper)

The paper in this book meets the guidelines for permanence and durability of the Committee on Production Guidelines for Book Longevity of the Council on Library Resources. ♾

Contents

Foreword

A View of the Adventure-Style Playgrounds of Central Park

I am honored to be asked to introduce this book on the adventure-style playgrounds of Central Park. It has been a while since I traveled this road, and it is a pleasure to gather my thoughts about a process in which I played a role and to glance back at the time when discovery and invention were encouraged.

To begin, let us recall that it was only after World War II that significant interest in play environments emerged. The Depression was over, and American cities were evolving from manufacturing centers to service centers sustained by an educated workforce with specialized skills. Urban families were smaller than before and enjoyed the benefits of discretionary time and increasing affluence. As one would expect, parents took an interest in the development and advancement of their children. At the same time, developmental psychology was discovering that early childhood was not just the dormant period before maturity and productivity, and that, in fact, the first five-to-ten years are the most influential in a child's social and cognitive development. The more stimulating the environment the child experienced, the greater the chances for a healthy and successful life.

It soon become clear that New York's Robert Moses–era playgrounds, often sterile, fenced, paved, and sparsely furnished places—custodial cages for kids—were not the stimulating environments that the times demanded. The belief was that such places would stunt rather than aid in childhood development. Pressure mounted for an alternative approach, ultimately resulting in the "playground revolution" and the designed landscapes this book is helping us remember and value. To meet the new challenge, and lacking any precedents, the design profession took an empirical approach based on experimentation, invention, and exploration. Central Park became (and remains) a testing ground, with a range of interesting, innovative, and creative play spaces that broke the mold. These designed landscapes were visually attractive to adults and engaging to children, forming a typology that is commonly called adventure-style playgrounds.

When the adventure-style playgrounds came to the fore, there were two distinctly different philosophies on how to provide for play: "product" and "process." European adventure playgrounds (where the label "adventure-style" playground originated) focused on process, a hands-on experience, overseen by a play leader, in which the children conceived and constructed environments with real tools and random materials. In this way, children were the creators of their playgrounds, with the underlying adventure being the experience of designing and constructing. The "process" approach thus developed social, collaborative, cooperative, and mechanical skills, while fostering enjoyment, self-confidence, pride, and problem-solving. Adventure-style playgrounds in America, however, focused on product, which meant creating a fixed, designed environment offering choice, challenge, and interpretation. United States cities preferred this approach because it was less costly and involved less liability, and it did not require the ongoing management of the more logistically complex aspects of the "process" approach.

The adventure-style playgrounds in Central Park and elsewhere were rich in opportunities, yet almost all, paradoxically, were enclosed by seven-foot-high chain-link or cast-iron fences (some with spiked pickets). A persistent holdover from the "Moses cage," such fences enclosed the play area and tacitly implied that, upon entering the gated precinct, *play begins,* and upon exiting, *play ceases.* Although responding to the need for secure and safe play, the fences were nonetheless an overbearing means of control that contradicted the underlying intention of the experience, which was to create a child's precinct where exploration, imagination, and awareness are encouraged. They also communicated that play was to be contained and is not an integral part of daily activity. The lesson here is to understand that the way we physically define the boundaries of play deserves the same creative consideration as the play space itself. Even so, the adventure-style playgrounds were and are a commendable demonstration of how the designed environment can respond to and complement the findings of the behavioral disciplines.

And yet we seem to have reached a plateau in that regard. History and religion have long devalued play as a limited, unproductive activity restricted to children. It is likewise a commonly held view that adult play exists primarily within the arena of competitive sports and games. But psychologists have shown how skills, understanding, and self-realization are developed and enhanced through abstraction, imagination, and experimentation—in other words, through *play.* If play enhances understanding and enjoyment for adults, then why should it be restricted to children? It may take a cultural revolution of sorts to change such attitudes, but many adults who enjoy and value existential experiences are already among us. Although the artist, musician, or mountain climber does not readily describe what they do as play (likely for fear of being stigmatized by that word), what they do really *is* play. For example, I often say that I am "going to work," but what I am really doing is "going to play," because I take great pleasure in what I do. We seem to regard "going to play" with suspicion, and yet we often repeat the Chinese proverb that says, "If you like what you do, you will never work a day in your life."

Returning to Central Park, the adventure-style playgrounds there are part of an iconic, Olmsted-designed landscape that offers much more than beautiful scenic views. The rock outcroppings, bosques of trees, lakes, ponds, and passing pedestrians comprise a living narrative replete with subplots of water mirroring the clouds and stars, the wind's angry and soothing moods, the sun's marking the hours and seasons, and shadows creating transient art. My own connection to Olmsted was forged in the park when, in the mid-1980s, I designed the East 67th Street Playground (a.k.a. the Billy Johnson Playground), the first playground reconstructed under the administration of the Central Park Conservancy. My goal was to create a natural rather than an urban experience, using the park's rustic vocabulary in a setting that echoed the surrounding topography—the lighter the touch, the better. The rich physical context of Olmsted's design continues to afford ample opportunities for the curious, and we should continue to strive to integrate the designed play environments with the nature that fills the park—to connect the "adventure" in the playgrounds to the park itself.

Doing so fully may entail another revolution in which we fundamentally reconceive what it means to play, as well as who plays and where. Could we experience work and education as play rather than as chores? Does play really come down to a state of mind? Until we are prepared to answer such questions, we may have to be content to make smaller strides in design within the restrictive definition of play spaces. In the meantime, we would do well to remember that adventure is not to go where no others have been, but to go where *you* have *not* been. For those who are curious, that might just be through the opening in a seven-foot-high barrier.

M. Paul Friedberg, FASLA

Editor's Introduction

Valuing a Layered Design Legacy

Welcome to the third publication in the *Modern Landscapes: Transition and Transformation* series. This volume takes a fresh look at the iconic Central Park, but instead of the picturesque landscape designed by Frederick Law Olmsted and Calvert Vaux based on their competition-winning "Greensward" plan of 1858, it focuses on the lesser-known period when modernism began to take hold in New York and in the park, contributing to the radical transformation of many of its playgrounds. *Central Park's Adventure-Style Playgrounds: Renewal of a Midcentury Legacy* documents the design trends, social motivations, and public engagement that made the park a kind of laboratory for playground design from 1967 to 1979. It was during this period that the park's existing playgrounds—collections of isolated play equipment set on asphalt pavement behind iron fences—were reborn as comprehensively designed environments where interconnected forms, such as pyramids, mounds, and steps, and basic materials, such as water and sand, encouraged new levels of creativity and interaction.

Architect Richard Dattner, who created six of the new playgrounds, summed up the philosophy behind his work: "The environment for play must be rich in experience, and it must be, to a significant extent, under the control of the child." Responding to new attitudes and expectations about children's play, Dattner's designs were a synthesis of European adventure playgrounds, innovative landforms reminiscent of the work of artist Isamu Noguchi, and groundbreaking playgrounds designed by landscape architect M. Paul Friedberg. Beyond their functional role, the new play environments added another layer to the park's rich design legacy and thus entered into dialogue with Olmsted and Vaux. By foregrounding an important aspect of the park's twentieth-century history, we can gain new insight into that conversation and add to our understanding of Central Park as a whole.

Chronicling multiple sites within Central Park, the present volume (the first with Louisiana State University Press in the series) differs somewhat from its predecessors, which were dedicated to individual landscapes: Lawrence Halprin's Skyline Park in Denver, Colorado (completed in 1975), and John Simonds's Mellon Square in Pittsburgh, Pennsylvania (completed in 1955). *Skyline Park,* published in 2012, was written in response to the site's controversial 2003 overhaul when much of Halprin's design was demolished and a Historic American Landscapes Survey (HALS) was undertaken to document the park prior to its alteration (the first such recordation effort for a modernist work of landscape architecture in the United States). *Mellon Square,* a much happier story, was published in 2015 following the plaza's complete revitalization by the Pittsburgh Parks Conservancy. The book is a case study that chronicles the research, analysis, and results of a collaborative undertaking between a client and a design team whose goal was to restore an exemplary modernist work of landscape architecture. The project is a remarkable example of what can be achieved when one generation strives to understand the design intent of another.

The need for intergenerational stewardship brings us back to Central Park and the work of the Central Park Conservancy, founded in 1980. In its early days, the conservancy was faced with the mammoth task of rescuing and rebuilding much of the park. The innovative modernist playgrounds—and all the park's playgrounds for that matter—were not the utmost priority, even though, like many works of postwar landscape architecture, they were suffering from years of deferred maintenance and deterioration. With new concerns about playground safety overshadowing the value of the acclaimed designs, some of the playgrounds were threatened with outright destruction.

But in the late 1990s, the conservancy began to update the modernist playgrounds, responding in large measure to a grassroots movement aimed at preserving them. As with many of the stories of modernist landscape architecture, the public call to action compelled the conservancy to balance change and preservation as part of its work in the park, ultimately adding to its reputation as a model champion of innovative park stewardship in the United States. In its 2011 publication *Plan for Play: A Framework for Rebuilding and Managing Central Park Playgrounds,* the conservancy summarizes its approach to the stewardship of playgrounds, noting that "while their purpose and essential premise has remained consistent, playgrounds are constantly refined and reinvented to reflect evolving ideas and contemporary expectations about children's needs and the role of play."

The present publication illustrates just such a reinvention in response to evolving expectations, as well as the balancing act that designers and stewards must engage in to ensure the health, safety, and welfare of the public—a process made no easier by the fact that Central Park, the epitome of nineteenth-century landscape architecture in the United States, is also a National Historic Landmark and a global destination. In a 2008 interview, M. Paul Friedberg (standing in Central Park's Billy Johnson Playground, which he designed in the 1980s) summed up the challenge of adding a new layer to the revered landscape by Olmsted and Vaux: "It was the lighter the touch, the better . . . the obligation went back, as well as forward."

As *Central Park's Adventure-Style Playgrounds* demonstrates, the commitment to look "back, as well as forward," to use Friedberg's simple but profound words, is not only a commitment to wise stewardship, it is also foundational to the quest for exemplary design.

Charles A. Birnbaum, FASLA, FAAR

Central Park's Adventure-Style Playgrounds

Introduction

While Central Park is one of the most important public spaces in the world, and its influence on landscape architecture and public park development have been well-established, the park's role in the history of innovative playground design is little known. The park is still home to some of the playgrounds built during the mid-1960s and early 1970s as part of a widespread movement to reimagine the urban playground. The landscape architects, architects, and artists who designed playgrounds during this period broke from the long-standing conception of the playground as a collection of manufactured equipment and, for the first time, created unique play environments that incorporated topography, sculptural features, and a variety of materials for children to manipulate. These playgrounds were a response to new ideals for children's play that emerged in the years after World War II, as well as to the precarious state of the American city in the 1960s. The intent of these playgrounds to promote an engaged exploration of space and form that would enliven the senses and stimulate the imagination reflected a heightened interest in cultivating creativity in children. Enriching opportunities for play through innovative design was also an attempt to elevate the role of recreation in public life and as vehicle for urban revitalization. Drawing from the rhetoric and spirit of the 1960s counterculture, designers, park administrators, and the press declared the movement a "playground revolution."

The playground revolution began and flourished in New York and resulted in a remarkably dense concentration of examples in Central Park. By the end of the 1970s, a total of ten of the park's twenty-two existing playgrounds—equipment-filled lots dating to the 1930s—had been transformed according to the new ideals of design. [FIG. 1] Architect Richard Dattner designed the first of these playgrounds in Central Park, called Adventure Playground, which opened in 1967 to wide acclaim and became a model for playgrounds citywide. [FIGS. 2 AND 3] This success led Dattner, who had never designed a playground before, to become one of the

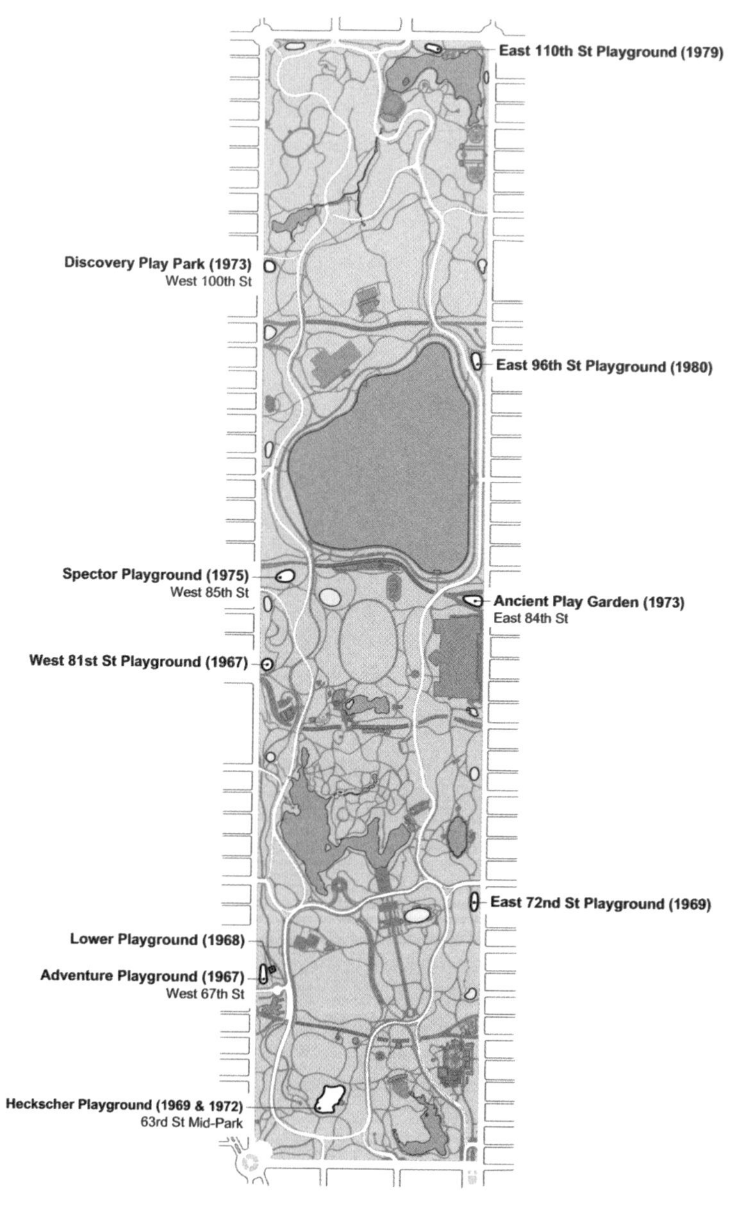

FIG. 1
Central Park playgrounds rebuilt between 1967 and 1980.

FIG. 2
West 67th Street Playground, Central Park, 1966.
The playground that preceded Adventure Playground was typical of those throughout Central Park and New York, comprised of standard equipment on an asphalt ground.

movement's leaders and to contribute a total of six playgrounds to the collection in Central Park.

Dattner embarked on his first project in Central Park by closely studying earlier groundbreaking design concepts and theories about play and child development, both of which had contributed to a renewal of interest in children's play environments. He was particularly drawn to playgrounds developed in postwar Europe, which contained no equipment or designed features but instead involved adults encouraging children to build with tools and materials. Known as adventure playgrounds, they inspired the name of Dattner's first playground and his goal to promote a more creative and exploratory play experience. However, Dattner's playground was a comprehensively designed space, and while this was the direction taken by other American designers of this period, the name "adventure playground," with its connotations of radicalism and innovation, became associated with the designed playgrounds of this era, now typically called "adventure-style playgrounds."

Beyond its example of innovative design, Adventure Playground in Central Park provided another revolutionary model—for the role of citizens

FIG. 3
Adventure Playground, 1967. Richard Dattner called his first playground a "playscape," a unique landscape for children's play.

in the process of creating playgrounds. Mothers living on the Upper West Side who had been pressuring the city's Parks Department for a safer and updated playground for several years set the project in motion and shepherded its design. A philanthropic foundation interested in revitalizing the city's playgrounds funded the cost. Ongoing citizen activism and investment was the force behind the proliferation of new playgrounds in Central Park and was indicative of broader trends. In 1966 one journalist observed, "Every second or third block seems to have its committee of militant mothers trying to raise money or enthusiasm for new playgrounds."[1] Betraying widespread dissatisfaction with the state of the city's recreational spaces, these mothers were part of a growing movement of citizens demanding a voice in decisions about the built environment, stemming in part from journalist and activist Jane Jacobs's grassroots efforts to protect and revitalize the city's neighborhoods.

The new playgrounds in Central Park were also radical for their context. Whereas other examples of adventure-style playgrounds sited in plazas and schoolyards appeared integrated with their urban surroundings, in Central Park their monumental geometric forms were a jarring contrast to such a naturalistic setting. Stylistically, the adventure-style playgrounds are examples of modern landscape architecture. A corollary of modernism encompassing the design of landscapes post–World War II through the early 1970s, modern landscape architecture is generally characterized by the use of experimental materials and forms, often with a clear social purpose, and in engagement with other disciplines and art forms.[2] (Some scholars and journalists have also used the term "Brutalist" to describe adventure-style playgrounds because of their prominent use of concrete.) As the country's first large urban park and epitome of nineteenth-century park design, Central Park was an unsuspecting place for modernism.

Frederick Law Olmsted and Calvert Vaux designed Central Park in the mid-1850s as a response to unprecedented urban growth, which they feared was compromising public health and consuming open space without consideration for recreation.[3] They conceived of the park as a unified composition of various landscapes—meadows, woodlands, glades, lakes, streams—experienced by sight and movement, primarily through walking along winding paths and formal promenades, and also in carriages and on horseback. Their intent was to simulate a visit to an idealized version of the countryside as an antidote to urban life. [FIGS. 4–6] Contact with natural scenery and open space, they believed, would provide urban dwellers with a sense of physical and psychological escape that would improve the human condition and thus further the progress of the city. Central Park had an immediate and profound influence on the creation and design of municipal parks nationwide and inaugurated the profession of landscape architecture in the United States. Despite numerous changes to its design and periods of deterioration and decline, the park's purpose as a scenic retreat from the city largely endured, and by the mid-1960s this recreational ideal was experiencing a prominent revival.

The adventure-style playgrounds—installed just over a century after the park's creation—were a significant update, but one consistent with how changing ideas about recreation had impacted the park throughout its history. These playgrounds replaced those installed in the 1930s as part of a modernization of Central Park under the administration of Parks Commissioner Robert Moses (1934–60). The adventure-style playgrounds were, however, exceptional during the 1960s and 1970s, a period with little

FIG. 4
The Island in the Lake, ca. 1872. The largest of the four water bodies in Central Park, the Lake was a popular destination for experiencing picturesque scenery.

FIG. 5
North Meadow, ca. 1872. Meadows offered an experience of open, seemingly boundless space, which park designers intended as a contrast to the feeling of confinement in the city.

FIG. 6
The Ramble, 1905.
Olmsted and Vaux designed the woodland landscape known as the Ramble as an immersive experience of nature, evoking the scenery of places like the Catskill Mountains in upstate New York.

other new construction in the park. This era is primarily associated with the park's most devastating phase of decline and the beginnings of the citizen-led movement to recognize its historic and cultural value, both of which resulted in efforts to preserve and restore it. The playground revolution unfolded in Central Park during a pivotal moment in the park's history: the playgrounds were islands of modern design in the park, created at a time when park administrators and advocates were attempting to reassert its nineteenth-century roots.

The playground revolution was part of a larger effort in New York to revitalize parks and reaffirm the role of recreation in urban life. While it resulted in radically different forms, the movement drew from Olmsted and Vaux's conception of park design as an art form with a profoundly social purpose. John Lindsay, who was elected mayor of New York in 1966, upheld parks as a vital resource that had long been neglected and his focus on public spaces had a clear social and political agenda. Severely deteriorated and largely abandoned, parks and playgrounds had become prominent signs of a city in crisis, evidence of how the upheavals of physical decline, economic disinvestment, and demographic shifts were irrevocably transforming New York. According to a 1962 survey of New Yorkers, fear was the most prevalent association with parks.[4]

The Parks Department during Lindsay's tenure, led first by Commissioner Thomas Hoving (1966–67) and then by August Heckscher (1967–72), championed innovative design, new uses for parks, and experiments in cultural programming as a way to reclaim and reinvigorate the public realm. [FIG. 7] They envisioned converting the city's many vacant lots into vest pocket parks, redeveloping the waterfront for recreational uses, and utilizing streets as venues for concerts and performances.[5] As part of broader efforts to provide more services to the poor, park administrators targeted neighborhoods lacking recreational opportunities, particularly those becoming notorious for crime and unrest. They were also hopeful that new recreational amenities and a vibrant cultural scene would help stem the exodus of middle- and upper-class residents to the suburbs. Dattner and the other leading playground designer of this period, landscape architect M. Paul Friedberg, furthered this notion of design as an instrument of social change through their built works as well as in their books, which functioned both as catalogs of their work and manifestos on urban recreation.[6] In 1972, *New York Magazine* heralded "adventure playgrounds" as one of the "101 Signs that the City Isn't Dying," indicative of how playgrounds were viewed as bright spots in an otherwise bleak urban scene.[7] Parks and playgrounds became the cornerstones to Mayor Lindsay's vision for a revitalized and more inclusive city. They demonstrated the value of the city itself.

This visionary program for parks and recreation was ultimately short-lived and largely unrealized in its time. Mounting urban problems and limited funds thwarted most of the ambitious schemes and compromised the Parks Department, leading to the citywide deterioration of parks, including the acclaimed adventure-style playgrounds. As the condition of Central Park worsened during the 1970s, the city's attention and the public's interest shifted from innovative playgrounds to the park. The work of concerned citizens and government officials strategizing ways to rescue Central Park resulted in the formation in 1980 of the Central Park Conservancy, a public-private partnership created to provide citizen leadership and invest private funds into the park's restoration and management. The organization's initial focus was the monumental task of restoring the park's

FIG. 7

Opening of vest pocket park on East 102nd Street, 1968. Epitomizing the city's goals for urban recreation during this period were small parks with adventure-style play features sited on vacant lots. Mayor John Lindsay is pictured in the center, with Parks Commissioner August Heckscher to his right.

landscapes and rebuilding its infrastructure, guided by the original design and vision of Olmsted and Vaux.

Central Park's collection of adventure-style playgrounds did not become a source of interest until the early 1990s, when plans to upgrade Adventure Playground inspired a debate about its value as a historic designed landscape worthy of preservation. No one had ever preserved a playground before; they had been consistently overhauled according to prevailing ideas about children's play, and historic preservation in Central Park had been primarily focused on Olmsted and Vaux's design. With pressure from advocates intent on reviving interest in the forgotten playground revolution, the conservancy began to consider ways to reconcile preservation with the need to update the playground to reflect contemporary ideas about children's recreation and standards for safety, which had become the driving force in new playground design since the 1980s. Over the course of several projects in adventure-style playgrounds since the early 2000s, the conservancy has honed an approach to these rare surviving playgrounds that prioritizes their value as functional play spaces while seeking to maintain their unique architectural and spatial character—ultimately upholding their original purpose to inspire a rich and engaging play experience. [FIG. 8]

Since the early 2000s, adventure-style playgrounds have experienced a revival, receiving attention from scholars, journalists, and curators.[8] This interest has emerged from diverse disciplines and topics: from a critical examination of contemporary playground design, to a focus on New York in the 1960s and 1970s, to histories of modern design for children. Most treatments of the adventure-style playgrounds focus on the design and designers of various playgrounds and the immediate cultural context in which they were created.

This book, which examines the adventure-style playgrounds in Central Park, has involved a more expansive approach that seeks to examine these playgrounds from the perspective of the park. It focuses on Central Park because the range of examples within the park, including some of the most illustrious, provides new insight into how the playground revolution originated and evolved. This exceptional concentration resulted from the sustained attention of city officials, mothers, and philanthropists, all of whom sought to invest in playgrounds—as well as in the city's premier public space. This public engagement in planning for the park's playgrounds influenced thinking about the stewardship of the entire park and ultimately

FIG. 8
Adventure Playground, 2015. The Central Park Conservancy updated Adventure Playground in 1997 and again in 2015.

the development of the Central Park Conservancy and its influential public-private partnership model.

The book also aims to show how the history and design of Central Park, as well as the culture of the park during the 1960s and 1970s, shaped the creation and experience of adventure-style playgrounds in ways that further elucidate their role in childhood and urban life. The result is a series of interweaving histories that trace the relationship of playgrounds to Central Park and the relationship of playgrounds to New York. To provide a greater understanding of the playground as an urban form and to set the stage for revolution, chapter 1 presents the origins of playgrounds and their history in New York and Central Park through the 1950s. Chapter 2 focuses on the playground revolution, analyzing Central Park's Adventure Playground—one of the earliest and most representative examples—as a vehicle for defining the movement. Chapter 3 explores how the movement evolved in Central Park through examples of additional playgrounds by Dattner and others, as well as new types of equipment that incorporated the ongoing development of ideas about design for play. This chapter reveals how the playgrounds' relationship to their setting was unexpectedly dynamic; more than just objects of modern design overlaid on the historic park, the playgrounds and the park were intertwined as participants in a process of reaffirming the role of recreation in urban life.

This history provides the foundation for the other topic of this book—the preservation and stewardship of adventure-style playgrounds as examples of modern landscape architecture and as spaces for children's play in Central Park. Chapter 4 charts the decline of the playgrounds and their resurgence stemming from community interest, which led to the development of an approach to their renewal. Examples of the conservancy's work evince the tension between preservation and modernization typical of many examples of historic preservation but present the particular challenges unique to playgrounds as well as to Central Park as one of the most heavily used public spaces in New York. These projects involve a process of preserving and building on the successful aspects of their designs while incorporating new technologies, materials, and equipment that reflect contemporary ideas about children's play and approaches to urban park management. They also involve updating the playgrounds of an earlier era in the context of the safety and accessibility standards that have evolved since their original construction. The Central Park Conservancy is well known for rescuing the park from the worst period of decline in its history and for its ongoing work restoring and managing the park, but what this process entails is still somewhat obscure. A focus on the stewardship of playgrounds provides new insight into the practices of landscape architecture, historic preservation, and park management in Central Park.

This book is an outgrowth of my experiences as director of preservation planning for the Central Park Conservancy and specifically my work on *Plan for Play,* a planning document created in 2011 to provide a framework for rebuilding and managing all of Central Park's playgrounds.[9] The first comprehensive examination of playgrounds as a distinctly modern layer of the park, this study involved the first deep investigation of their history, which led to reflection on the work updating adventure-style playgrounds in the context of this history and as part of the work restoring the park over a thirty-year period. This process of deeper thinking about adventure-style playgrounds further illuminated their enduring value, clarifying the reasons it was important to invest in their renewal and providing the inspiration for this book. Central Park's adventure-style playgrounds were exceptional as works of design that broke from the traditional mold and in doing so became striking material embodiments of the highest urban ideals, emphasizing the essential value of playgrounds as spaces that cultivate a child's innate desires to play and explore and as centers of community life and culture. Their strong social purpose still resonates, and the rich and immersive experience of play that they inspired has value for children decades later. The conservancy's work updating the adventure-style playgrounds has introduced them to new generations of children and park users, reaffirming their valuable contribution to the history of play and recreation in Central Park and New York.

1

The Playgrounds of the Past

Designers and park administrators often defined adventure-style playgrounds by the dramatic ways they deviated from the recreational spaces of the past. When in 1966 Parks Commissioner Thomas Hoving declared that Adventure Playground in Central Park was a "radical departure . . . from the junk we've had all these years," he was making a pointed critique of the standardized designs of playgrounds created during the lengthy administration of Commissioner Robert Moses.[1] Between 1934 and 1960, the Moses-led Parks Department greatly expanded the recreational landscape of New York; one of its most transformative achievements—and acclaimed in its time—was the creation of over six hundred playgrounds, twenty-two of which were found in Central Park.

While Hoving's denouncement of the past promoted what was a truly novel approach to playground design, the purpose and form of the urban playground had undergone earlier transformations. The creation of specialized environments for children's play derives from the understanding of childhood as a stage of life that requires protection, nurturing, and education, which emerged in Europe during the seventeenth and eighteenth centuries. Using this conception of childhood as a consistent framework, designers, artists, educators, and those involved in the welfare of children have frequently re-envisioned these spaces according to changing ideas of children's education, health, and recreation.[2] The history of playgrounds, beginning with the first spaces for children's play in Central Park, demonstrates this trajectory and serves as a foundation for understanding what made the adventure-style playgrounds not only a manifestation of cyclical change in design for play, but a completely new direction.

Design historians and others writing about adventure-style playgrounds typically do not discuss earlier playgrounds in much detail, and this omission is telling. This chapter shows how the original concept for the playground was to protect children from the dangers of urban life and prepare them for success in the modern world. These goals were furthered by the layout of the playground space and the individual pieces of equipment, but most directly by the involvement of adults organizing play. As primarily a social program supported but not defined by design, these playgrounds do not quite fit into design-centered narratives. The adventure-style playgrounds were revolutionary because of their design, but more precisely because they featured design so prominently and as the primary means of play.

This brief history also explains the origins of playgrounds and chronicles their constant role but changing meaning in urban life. In 1966, one of the mothers demanding a new playground in Central Park attempted to define the playground and underscore its utmost consequence: "A New York City playground can never be 'just' a playground; in a city where there are no back-yards, where children can't play on the street, have no hiding places or tree houses, the playground is their recreation world."[3] As a distinctly urban space, the playground is inextricably tied to ideas about the city, to its ambitions and vicissitudes. Playgrounds are a child's "recreation world" and the spatial and material manifestation of ideas about childhood, but they also transcend their fenced boundaries to become powerful symbols of the city's well-being and aspirations. In Central Park, where the creation of playgrounds was a source of tension and debate, they were additionally defined by their relationship to the park's original design and purpose.

Play in Central Park

When New York's leaders began planning Central Park in the early 1850s, the word "playground" had a much broader and more literal definition, without the exclusive associations with children and childhood. It referred to a ground for play, for field games such as baseball or cricket, for both adults and children. In 1858 the city organized a design competition for its first large urban park, which stipulated the inclusion of playgrounds, reflecting the growing popularity of organized sports.[4] Frederick Law Olmsted and Calvert Vaux included three such playgrounds in their winning entry from 1858, entitled "Greensward."

Central Park ultimately included only one playground—an open lawn in the park's southeast corner, intended for use by ball clubs organized by and for adult men. In 1861, after receiving an overwhelming number of applications from clubs to use the space, called the Playground or Ballground, the Board of Commissioners (the park's administrators) decided to restrict its use to children.[5] In an early articulation of the park's purpose, the commissioners had stipulated that "sports, games and parades, in which comparatively few can take part, will only be admissible in cases where they may be supposed to contribute indirectly to the pleasure of a majority of those visiting the Park."[6] The intensity and exclusivity of use by ball clubs was inconsistent with the park's purpose as an experience of landscape and a retreat from the city. Limiting use of the Playground to children, a group that was easier to manage, would enable the commissioners to maintain the lawn as a scenic landscape for all park visitors to enjoy.

The park's designers further supported this decision through their definition of the park as a "work of art," a unified composition wherein each detail was conscripted to contribute. In Olmsted's words, the park was "subject to the primary law of every work of art, namely, that it shall be framed upon a single, noble motive, to which the design of all its parts, in some more or less subtle way, shall be confluent and helpful."[7] They considered all non-landscape features—buildings, bridges, concessions—"accessory elements" and designed them to be secondary to landscape and supportive of scenic experience. This conception also informed their resistance to proposals for monuments, popular amusements, and elaborate gateways, which they deemed urban intrusions in a place intended as the city's antithesis.

The commissioners' solution to managing the Playground—reserving its use for another exclusive group—initially seems inconsistent with their democratic ideal. However, they upheld children as special visitors; as the park took shape, the commissioners and designers began to consider how to accommodate the needs of children within the framework of the park's purpose. "[Children] represent larger and deeper interests than any other class," they declared, and benefits to them—of fresh air, exercise, and play—therefore "become at once general and not exclusive."[8] Investment in the health and well-being of the city's youngest citizens furthered the purpose of the park to cultivate a great metropolis. The arrangement for children to use the Playground was made in collaboration with the Board of Education; at a time when school buildings did not include spaces for play and exercise, the park was their schoolyard and gymnasium. [FIG. 9]

FIG. 9
Central Park's first "Playground," 1869. The Playground was one of the earliest examples of how park administrators attempted to integrate and regulate active use in a landscape designed primarily for a passive, scenic experience.

The commissioners initially made this arrangement only for boys, but in 1867 they designated a separate playground, near 72nd Street and Fifth Avenue, for girls.[9]

In 1872, Olmsted and Vaux completed the "Children's District," a landscape they designed purposefully for young children that further revealed how they hoped children would benefit from the park. They located the Children's District near the Playground in the park's southeast corner to be accessible to main entrances and chose a somewhat secluded landscape bounded by large rock outcrops. The landscape's focal point was the Dairy, a neo-Gothic building reminiscent of a Swiss chalet. Intended as a concession, it sold fresh milk, at that time not readily available in the city, and other refreshments to young visitors. [FIG. 10] The Kinderberg Shelter was also striking, a large wood structure built on a massive rock outcrop that provided an airy prospect for picnics and games and a place "for toddling infants to practice their first steps."[10] [FIG. 11] The open lawn in front of the Dairy was intended for play: it hosted wooden swings and seesaws, the only examples of such equipment, and was also a space for children to "tumble about when sunshine favors."[11] [FIG. 12] Olmsted and Vaux designed the Children's District as a microcosm of the park, a country retreat for young children, with every detail conveying rusticity and salubriousness.

FIG. 10
The Dairy, ca. 1872.
Presiding over the Children's District, the Dairy was a clear declaration of investment in children that corresponded to the park's overall purpose to benefit public health.

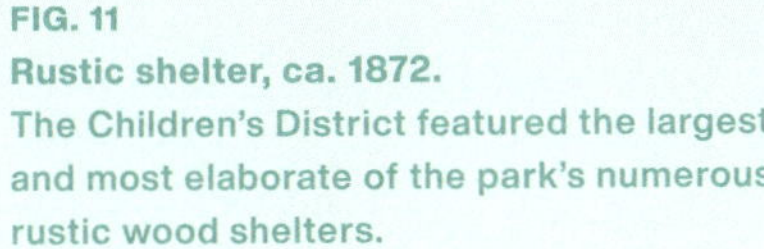

FIG. 11
Rustic shelter, ca. 1872.
The Children's District featured the largest and most elaborate of the park's numerous rustic wood shelters.

FIG. 12
Swing set in the Children's District, ca. 1872. Park administrators installed swings as temporary features.

FIG. 13
Boy in Central Park, 1863.
While the park's designers recognized the value of specialized spaces for children's play and exercise, they believed children could also benefit from the experience of the park's landscapes.

The playgrounds for boys and girls and the Children's District were the first public landscapes created specifically for children's use and enjoyment in New York. One journalist marveled at the park's collective offerings for children, which also included a carousel and a small menagerie: "The Central Park is the only place, excepting our public schools, where the interests of children had been made of paramount importance."[12] Creating these spaces emphasized that children were part of the public for which the park was created. Although the park's distance from the centers of population made it difficult for all children to reach, Central Park nonetheless set a precedent for the responsibility of public parks to provide for and nurture the city's youngest citizens. [FIG. 13]

The Playground Movement

The creation of Central Park was a response to urban growth, and as this continued unchecked into the twentieth century, concerns about its disastrous effects on public health and the continuing loss of open space led to new types of public spaces. The concept of the playground as a dedicated space for children's play emerged during the turn of the twentieth century in response to concerns about the effects of urbanization on children, particularly those living in slum neighborhoods.[13] As a broad network of citizens and civic leaders began to address the city's growing social and

FIG. 14
Byron Company, "The close of a career in New York," ca. 1900. This photograph of children playing in the gutter alongside a dead horse captures exactly why reformers were so concerned about street play.

environmental problems, many became particularly focused on children's health and education. For these urban reformers, children playing in the streets, in many neighborhoods the only available space for play, epitomized the failure of the city to provide for its citizens. [FIG. 14] Although the chaos of the streets may have been alluring to children, reformers saw them endangered by traffic and unsanitary conditions, crowded out by commerce, and exposed to immoral activities such as gambling, drinking, and fighting. Reformers redefined the playground as an alternative environment for play and made it a critical piece in a comprehensive program to transform urban childhood. Playgrounds were part of an expanding public landscape for children, one that consisted of other specialized spaces and buildings such as kindergartens, schools, orphanages, and summer camps.

The first manifestation of this goal to control the location and character of urban play was the sandbox, an idea and form that originated

FIG. 15
Jacob Riis, Sand Pile at Riverside Buildings, Brooklyn, ca. 1895. The creation of sand piles, also known as sand gardens, were the first efforts to organize and contain children's play.

FIG. 16
Playground on the Lower East Side, ca. 1898. Reformers built the city's first playgrounds as temporary projects on vacant lots.

FIG. 17
Seward Park, ca. 1905.
The playground and the adjacent bathhouse were the focal point of this and other small parks.

in Germany.[14] The sandbox (also called a sand garden) engaged children while facilitating their close supervision and ultimately established containment as essential to the design and program of the playground, a spatial paradigm that has endured.[15] [FIG. 15] During the 1890s in New York, reformers expanded the scale and scope of this concept by converting empty lots into spaces for play, incorporating equipment and open space for games, all protected from the street by fences. [FIG. 16]

In the same decade, New York's Parks Department, which was formed in the 1870s following the creation of Central Park to oversee and develop other open spaces, began building small neighborhood parks, to provide more accessible recreational opportunities.[16] By the early twentieth century, pressure from reformers and playground advocates, led the city to begin to incorporate playgrounds into these parks. The city's first playground was created in 1903 as part of Seward Park, a new park on the Lower East Side, one of the city's most densely populated neighborhoods.[17] [FIG. 17] Samuel Parsons Jr., a landscape architect who had worked for many years in Central Park and designed many small parks

FIG. 18
Playground, Thomas Jefferson Park, 1912. Gymnastic equipment was included in most early playgrounds, intended for use by both men and boys, and a precedent for the design of later jungle gyms.

during this period, attempted to integrate this modern facility within a more traditional park framework, surrounding the playgrounds with tree and shrub plantings. Despite Parsons's efforts to assert naturalistic landscaping, playgrounds and park buildings were the most prominent features of most small parks. The playground included ample open space for games—still functioning as a ground for play—but newly included various types of equipment, such as gymnastic apparatus, swings, seesaws, merry-go-rounds, and slides. [FIG. 18] Park structures ranged from simple shade structures to elaborate open-air pavilions and bathhouses designed in the Beaux Arts style, bestowing these new public spaces with civic grandeur. During the early twentieth century, many parks also included gardens in which Parks Department employees provided instruction to children on how to grow vegetables and flowers on their own plots.[18] The didactic purpose of the gardens was aligned with that of playgrounds, whose success, advocates believed, was contingent on adult supervision and instruction. Parks Department employees known as "play leaders" supervised play and organized events and games, which they infused with a moral value system intended to instill concepts of cooperation, industriousness, and civic pride and often targeted to immigrant children as a form of acculturation. While the civilizing function of parks had been central to the ideology of Frederick Law Olmsted and other mid-nineteenth century park advocates, the process by which this was achieved in a space like Central Park—through enjoyment of nature and landscape scenery—was more indirect. The seriousness of the activity on the playground—and its implications for the future of the city—was expressed in the unofficial slogan of the playground movement: "The boy without a playground is the father to the man without a job."[19]

No playgrounds, according to the twentieth-century definition of an enclosed space with equipment and other facilities for children, were built in Central Park until 1926, but it was not immune to the influence of the playground movement. The park was the setting for many organized events for children—athletic competitions, historic pageants, and performances of folk dancing, programming typical of playgrounds citywide.[20] Most of these events took place on the Sheep Meadow, the park's southernmost open lawn. [FIGS. 19 AND 20] Occurring in a space without any equipment or facilities, these events demonstrated how the playground was actually a flexible concept, determined more by ideology and program than by design and site.

Ideas about the preservation and management of Central Park informed the creation of its first playground. Called Heckscher Playground, it was created over twenty years after reformers had launched the playground movement and after many failed attempts by advocates and park administrators to build playgrounds in the park. Parks Commissioner Charles Stover (1910–13), formerly a settlement worker, was an ardent supporter of public playgrounds, including one controversial proposal from 1910 to convert Central Park's northernmost meadow into an extensive recreational complex with a swimming pool, tennis courts, and children's playgrounds.[21] Those protesting this and other proposals recognized the value of playgrounds but argued that the park was not an appropriate setting.[22] Landscape architect Downing Vaux (son of Calvert Vaux) declared, "People will forget that the Park is a place for rest. . . . It was never designed for a playground. . . . But it is a continuous struggle to keep that before the public mind."[23] Building playgrounds, protestors worried, would set a precedent for other additions to the park, a fear that was not unfounded. Since the park's creation, individuals and organizations had proposed myriad structures and facilities and such proposals increased during the early twentieth century, including suggestions for an outdoor theater, stadium, and opera house.[24] However, by the 1920s, growing use of the park—including the numerous events for children that left landscapes trashed and eroded—

FIG. 19
Sheep Meadow, ca. 1900. Still grazed by sheep in the early twentieth century, the Sheep Meadow was one of the park's most bucolic landscapes.

FIG. 20
May Day celebration on the Sheep Meadow, ca. 1910. The Sheep Meadow was also the location for numerous mass events for children, an example of how the playground movement affected the park.

FIG. 21
Bird's-eye-view of Central Park showing Heckscher Playground, 1927. The Parks Department built Heckscher Playground on a section of the original nineteenth-century Playground (the eroded lawn in center left).

FIG. 22
Wading pool, Heckscher Playground, 1932. The wading pool was one of the first in a city park, signaling Central Park's first playground as a truly modern facility.

shifted the perspective of playgrounds as a way to actually improve and protect the park by containing and controlling children's use.[25] The Parks Department constructed the Heckscher Playground near the park's southern border, providing a diverse array of amenities for children, including a wading pool, play equipment, open space for games, and a building with restrooms—all contained by a fence lined with trees and shrubs. [FIGS. 21 AND 22] Built with funds from the Heckscher Foundation, an organization created in 1921 to support child welfare causes, this playground was also one of the earliest examples of philanthropic investment in Central Park.

The success of Heckscher Playground inspired a visionary idea to further accommodate children's play in the park. In a report detailing the condition of the park, Hermann Merkel (a consulting landscape architect for the Parks Department) praised Heckscher Playground because it protected other landscapes from overuse. He suggested additional playgrounds, located adjacent to entrances and "so situated that they will not appear in any of the long views," to provide access to play without infringing on the park's overall design and experience.[26]

Modernizing Play

Building playgrounds was the initial focus of a massive expansion and modernization of the parks system orchestrated by Parks Commissioner Robert Moses beginning in 1934 with federal funding from the Works Progress Administration (WPA).[27] Drawing from the general design of earlier playgrounds, the Parks Department created a template of standardized features and amenities that was replicated throughout the city: swings, slides, seesaws, jungle gyms, sandboxes or sand-tables, sprinklers or wading pools, water fountains, benches, and fencing. [FIG. 23] Although these playgrounds later became associated primarily with this equipment, at the time of their creation, the play experience was not determined by equipment alone. Playgrounds continued to be overseen by play leaders, known in this period as playground directors, and were the stage for a range of programmed activities for children, including tournaments for sports and games; singing, dancing, and music contests; and magic and art shows.[28] In 1939 the Parks Department employed eight hundred playground directors for approximately four hundred playgrounds, indicative of the importance of programming and oversight; over half of these were relief workers, funded through the WPA.[29] Many playground activities aimed to provide social instruction, promoting values such as teamwork and cooperation, and playground directors played a similar role to that they had played in the past, ensuring that children were playing productively and safely. But the seriousness of play that characterized the early twentieth century, driven by the urban reform movement, had largely dissipated, and many programs were intended for entertainment or as an outlet for self-expression. Writing about New York's play facilities in 1937, one journalist exclaimed, "You've never seen anybody having as much fun as the children in this town are having."[30] By 1960, the Parks Department had built over six hundred play-

FIG. 23
Arnold Eagle, Federal Art Project, "Playground—Supervised Game 1," 1935. Adult supervision was central to the experience of the playgrounds constructed during the administration of Robert Moses.

grounds throughout the city, making them integral to the experience and fabric of urban life.[31]

While playgrounds were an initial focus of the Moses administration, they were ultimately just one type of facility in an expanding recreational landscape that included new parks, pools, and beaches, a public realm that signified New York's ascendance as a modern city. Beyond supporting population growth, this focus on recreation accommodated the growing interest in organized team sports and other leisure-time pursuits arising from various social and economic shifts, including shorter work schedules and earlier retirement ages. Building on the division of space for active and passive use articulated earlier in small parks, the new parks endeavored further containment of more activities and age groups: playgrounds for young children, open areas for sports for teenagers, and shaded areas with benches and game tables for adults. [FIG. 24] The Parks Department admitted their design standards were "conservative," declaring that facilities "must be usable and durable in the aesthetic as well as the physical sense."[32] However, not all recreational design

FIG. 24
Seward Park, 1941.
The Parks Department rebuilt Seward Park in the 1930s with areas for different uses and age groups separated from one another by chain-link fencing.

was standardized; as scholar Marta Gutman has shown, the Parks Department designed swimming pools as monumental structures with extraordinary attention to detail and style.[33]

Based on earlier recommendations of Hermann Merkel to provide carefully sited play areas for children and as part of a major effort to modernize and renovate Central Park, beginning in 1935 the Parks Department constructed eighteen playgrounds along the park's perimeter, designed by staff landscape architects and engineers. This momentous transformation was well covered in the city's newspapers, which highlighted the playgrounds' dual purpose in the park. One editorial summarized that the playgrounds "will intercept the little potential destroyers on the perimeter of the park, and so while providing play attractions for them will protect the natural beauty of the greater areas within."[34] The earlier dismissals of playgrounds as encroachments seem to have been forgotten—in part because the park had severely deteriorated.[35] Architecture critic Lewis Mumford, who remembered the park in the 1920s as like "a movie background of a shell-torn battle area," praised the recent investments, particularly the introduction of "popular touches" such as playgrounds, which he believed had been accomplished "without destroying the original atmosphere."[36] Although these playgrounds had the same features as those cropping up throughout the city and their modern, industrial materials contrasted with the surrounding park, their siting and design were sensitive to their context. They had round or oval footprints—organic shapes that corresponded to the park's naturalistic character—and were bounded by plantings, low fences, and rows of benches. [FIGS. 25 AND 26] But in 1937, a year after the playgrounds opened, the Parks Department began installing seven-foot-tall wrought iron fences with gates for enhanced security, specifically to protect young children from the more rambunctious activity of older children and prevent "vagrants" from entering at night.[37] This addition reinforced the notion of the urban playground as an inward-focused space designated as separate from its surroundings, which, in the park setting, the Parks Department had sought to break away from. [FIG. 27]

The Battle of Central Park

In 1956, a protest organized by a group of mothers, regular park users and residents of the Upper West Side, became a seminal moment for the history of Central Park. Known as "The Battle of Central Park," the protest was a response to the Parks Department's plans to expand the Tavern on the Green restaurant, specifically the construction of a parking lot on a shaded lawn adjacent to the playground located near West 67th Street.[38] (This playground was later rebuilt as Adventure Playground.) These mothers described the landscape slated for destruction as a "romping grounds" for older children that as a community gathering space was also "the center of our neighborhood."[39] When the mothers first expressed concern over these plans, the Parks Department ignored them—Moses asserted that the area had never been a play space—and went ahead with construction.[40] The mothers responded by standing guard at the site, physically blocking the work from continuing. [FIG. 28] Moses was unrelenting; after the project was stalled for a few days, he ordered the construction to begin again—this time in the middle of the night—resulting in the removal of numerous trees and shrubs. One of the protestors sued the city, and the case dragged on until unexpectedly, Moses offered a concession: the city would cancel its

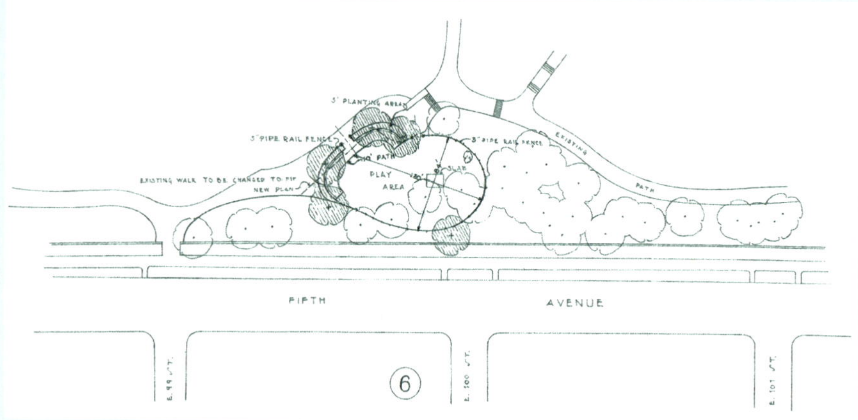

FIG. 25
Typical Central Park playground design, 1935. The Parks Department attempted to carefully interweave playgrounds into the landscapes along the park's perimeter.

FIG. 26
Perimeter playground at East 100th Street, 1936. The Parks Department originally designed playgrounds without fences, intending them to be open to the surrounding landscapes.

FIG. 27
Central Park playground at West 100th Street, 1959. While providing a safer environment for young children, the addition of fences made the playgrounds more disconnected from the rest of the park.

plans and build a new playground on the site of the partially built parking lot. This playground was completed in October, resulting in a strange configuration—a small rectangular playground (the footprint of the parking lot), directly adjacent to the existing oval-shaped playground. [FIG. 29]

The Battle of Central Park was remarkable for several reasons. The protest was part of a long history of citizens defending the park from encroachments but in retrospect, it anticipated the urgency and tenor of activism during the 1960s, which saw an increase in proposals for additions to the park. It called attention to women and mothers, typically unheard in debates over public space, who became increasingly vocal in the ensuing years and often specifically about spaces for children's play. It was also a rare citizen victory over the seemingly omnipotent Robert Moses that exposed the covert tactics of his Parks Department, marking the beginning of a precipitous decline in his public image. Lastly, the Battle of Central Park reinforced prevailing conceptions about playgrounds and their relationship to the park. Although the press portrayed the mothers as triumphant, and

FIG. 28
Battle of Central Park protest, 1956. Photographs of mothers blocking construction published in various newspapers thrust the protest into the spotlight.

FIG. 29
Playground created in the aftermath of the Battle of Central Park, 1957. Directly adjacent to an existing playground, the new playground appeared somewhat out of place and extraneous.

the mothers expressed pride in their success in thwarting the construction of the parking lot, they lost what they had actually been fighting for—a landscape composed of trees, grass, and rocks that also served as a play space for children. In treatments of this history, authors have consistently misinterpreted the mothers' fight as over an actual playground, perhaps also reflecting a lack of appreciation of landscape as play space.[41] Instead of restoring the landscape, the Parks Department presented the mothers and their children with a newly minted playground, reflecting the idea that play should occur in a specialized facility designated separate from the surrounding environment.

In October 1956, on the heels of the Battle of Central Park, another protest by mothers about a park playground did not receive nearly the same level of attention but was nonetheless significant as a window into the state of the city's playgrounds.[42] A group of mothers who lived near the northwest corner of the park and frequented a playground near West 110th Street protested Moses's announcement that the Parks Department lacked the resources to staff Central Park's playgrounds. Holding up signs reading "Attendants not Drunks," and "We Demand Protection," the mothers expressed concern for the safety of themselves and their children. Moses had built his reputation promoting and building playgrounds. Twenty years later, the city's mothers were publicly denouncing him as a destroyer of play space and accusing his administration of not fulfilling one of the critical functions of the playground—to keep children safe.

This situation was the culmination of a decade-long process of decline. The great expansion of the parks system, funded with federal relief money, was never followed up with adequate resources to sustain it. Following the diversion of funds and workers during World War II, staffing and programming had been gradually reduced while the conditions of playgrounds deteriorated.[43] This decline was exacerbated by Moses's shift in focus from recreational facilities to urban renewal and infrastructure projects. Revealing of its new priorities, in 1962 the Parks Department identified the construction of highways as "important sources for new playgrounds," which were built in the leftover spaces.[44]

The playground revolution in Central Park began in 1963, coincidentally in the same location as the Battle of Central Park, when a new generation of mothers formed a group called the Mothers Committee to Improve the West 67th Street Playground and began petitioning the Parks

FIG. 30
Rubber matting at the East 72nd Street Playground, 1969.
The installation of rubber matting was significant as the first update to the Moses-era playgrounds.

Department to make safety improvements to the playground after several of their children were injured.[45] The Parks Department did take action: they installed rubber mats under play equipment in this and other locations, with the ultimate goal of addressing all of the city's playgrounds, an effort they described as the "first major modernization of materials in the city's playgrounds in twenty-five years."[46] [FIG. 30] But this intervention did not alleviate all of the mothers' concerns. They asserted that the playground was "dull both physically and visually, and depressingly institutional" and demanded an entirely new playground—"an inviting and challenging playground which would delight and intrigue its users and be worthy of the City of New York."[47] They changed their name to the Committee for a Creative Playground to reflect these expanded aspirations.[48]

The playground revolution in New York was a response to the lack of attention to and deterioration of playgrounds, led by these and other mothers who were initially responding to concerns about safety. They began to focus on design of playgrounds—the ubiquitous equipment derided as "junk" by Commissioner Hoving in 1966—because without programming and staff, it was all that was left. The slides, seesaws, and swings—never intended as the sole source of play—were not only dilapidated and less safe without supervision but wholly inadequate in providing for children's recreational needs. As reflected in the mothers' choice of "creative," new ideals for children's play and recreation were beginning to influence their assessment of the playgrounds of the past and desires for the future.

2

Adventure Playground and the Playground Revolution

Adventure Playground, completed in May of 1967, was architect Richard Dattner's response to the demands of mothers to replace the Moses-era playground with an engaging and creative play space. Within the confines of the existing fence, Dattner designed play features inspired by natural and architectural forms, incorporating a pyramid, mound, amphitheater, tree house, and several small mazes, all set in a large expanse of sand. [FIG. 31] Unlike traditional play equipment, many of the features were interconnected and all could be experienced in a variety of ways. A low, undulating concrete wall wound around existing trees, integrating them into the design while also providing a place to sit and a form to walk along, jump from, or climb. The architect also enhanced the experience of water, which in most playgrounds was limited to a lone sprinkler. Water flowed into a large wading pool and then into a narrow channel along the center of the playground before ending in a smaller wading pool. [FIG. 32] If the playgrounds of the past were defined less by design than by programming, here design was paramount and its experience the main activity. Dattner called Adventure Playground "a landscape for the kids," defining the playground as a comprehensively designed environment and making a connection to its Central Park setting.[1]

Dattner's first playground drew from earlier attempts to expand the possibilities of playgrounds, which by the mid-1960s were coalescing into a true movement. The Park Association, a long-standing New York–based parks advocacy organization, made the first attempt to define the movement and give it a name. In a twenty-two-page booklet entitled "The Playground Revolution," published in October 1966, the organization documented various experimental attempts to reinvigorate the playground beginning in the early 1960s: new forms of play equipment and site furnishings, the addition of sculptures and murals, and the creation of new types of recreational spaces, such as vest pocket parks.[2] Based on these examples, the organization articulated a clear goal to build playgrounds that

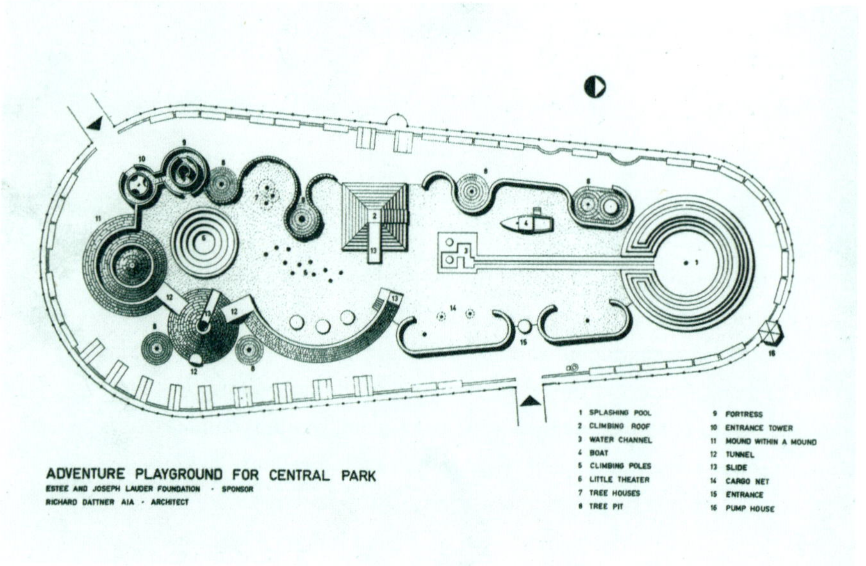

FIG. 31
Richard Dattner, plan for Adventure Playground, 1966. Dattner used low walls, tunnels, and steps to connect the various play features.

were "visually exciting, adapted to [their] environment and related to the needs of the community." It specified further that playgrounds needed to be safe, but most critically, they needed to "provide an outlet for imaginative and creative play."[3] Dattner closely studied many of the precedents documented in the booklet, and his first playground adhered to the Park Association's aspirations for new playgrounds to cultivate the creative child while being connected to the life of a neighborhood. He found the most direct models for his vision of the playground as a "landscape for the kids" in some of the designs of landscape architect M. Paul Friedberg as well as in the unrealized playground proposals by the artist Isamu Noguchi, both of whom approached the playground from different disciplines but arrived at a similar, and foundational, concept.

Dattner's involvement in this project arose because of the Parks Department's openness, beginning with the new administration in 1966, to not only new concepts for playgrounds but also the cultivation of new forms of citizen involvement in parks.[4] The latter was identified as essential by the Parks Association, who believed that the success of innovative playgrounds, which were more complicated and expensive to build and

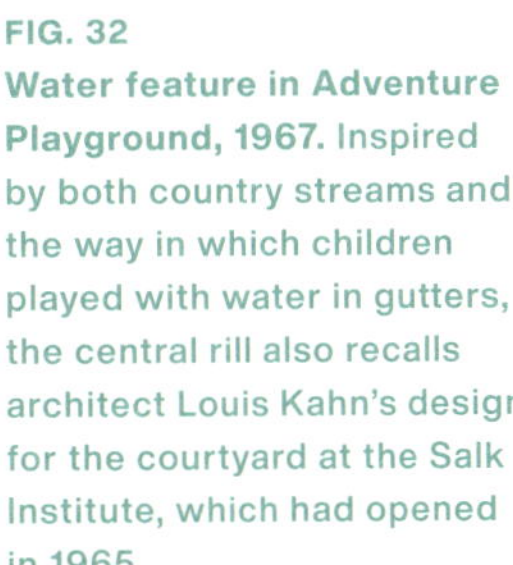

FIG. 32
Water feature in Adventure Playground, 1967. Inspired by both country streams and the way in which children played with water in gutters, the central rill also recalls architect Louis Kahn's design for the courtyard at the Salk Institute, which had opened in 1965.

maintain, was dependent on greater citizen participation in planning, financing, and management. Adventure Playground was a case in point: It was set in motion by neighborhood mothers and its $85,000 cost (significantly more than traditional playgrounds) was funded by the Lauder Foundation, a philanthropic organization started by Estée Lauder, founder of the successful beauty product company. [FIGS. 33 AND 34]

Park administrators encouraged the Lauders to bring on Dattner as the designer (they had worked with him previously on the design of the company's laboratories in 1964) and facilitated continued collaboration and communication between donor, architect, and the mothers' group.[5] Mrs. Lauder had created the foundation in 1962 with her husband, Joseph, "as a means of improving the quality of family life in the U.S."[6] They had approached the Parks Department with their first goal—to create and improve playgrounds—at the suggestion of their son Leonard, who had been stirred by the flight of friends to the suburbs due to growing concern about raising children in the city. "We decided to build several of these to give the

FIG. 33
Leonard Lauder, Thomas Hoving, Estee Lauder, Joseph Lauder, and Richard Dattner with model for Adventure Playground, 1966.
The city officially accepted the gift from the Lauders at an event in June 1966.

FIG. 34
Ruth Orkin, Groundbreaking for Adventure Playground, 1966.
The Committee for a Creative Playground, who had been petitioning for a new playground for three years, celebrated their victory at the groundbreaking in October 1966.

city just this little lift," Joseph explained, a declaration of the expanded role of playgrounds.[7] This confluence of participants with a united vision made Adventure Playground one of the most popular and acclaimed playgrounds from this period and a model for subsequent playgrounds in Central Park.[8] An analysis of the influences on the design of Adventure Playground reveals the constellation of ideas, projects, and people that shaped the playground revolution.

Learning from the Street

Dattner developed his concept for Adventure Playground through a close investigation of children's play in the urban environment. He documented this process in his 1969 book, *Design for Play,* marveling at how children were drawn to streets and empty lots because there they encountered various materials to manipulate and a sense of the unexpected, which were lacking in traditional playgrounds. [FIG. 35] Dattner's observations, while not new, were his window into play that became the starting point for a design approach that was more child-centered. If urban reformers had invented the playground as a retreat from the (urban) world, Dattner envisioned it as a microcosm, "with as many as possible of the sensory experiences to be found in the world included in it."[9] Guided by his wife, Shelly, who was studying child psychology, Dattner interpreted his findings through the theories of various psychologists, including Erik Erikson, Bruno Bettelheim, and Jean Piaget and concluded that the richness of experiences, interaction with one's environment, and some degree of control and independence were all critical for child development and should therefore be incorporated into the design of playgrounds.

Dattner's interest in the child's experience of the city and embrace of observation as a tool of design was indebted to Jane Jacobs's investigations of the social life of urban spaces in her book *The Death and Life of Great American Cities* (1961). Responding to the destruction of the city's historic neighborhoods in the name of urban renewal, she inveighed against planners and architects who failed to observe how cities actually worked, encouraging them to look closely at "the most ordinary scenes and events, and attempt to see what they mean."[10] She had come to a deeper understanding of urban life through studying older city districts and particularly through observing the street life in these neighborhoods. Street life, she discovered, was the "art form of the city," most comparable to dance,

FIG. 35
Katrina Thomas, Children playing in lot on East 6th Street, 1968. Although garbage-strewn lots were far from ideal as play spaces, they were attractive to children because of the range of materials to interact with.

encompassing the mundane and the dramatic, public activities and private life, in an "intricate ballet" that animated a neighborhood.[11]

As the stage for public neighborhood life, Jacobs found that the street had specific value for children. Busy sidewalks, aside from offering endless stimulation for children, were often safer than spaces designated for play because the critical mass of adults provided a "casual surveillance," a collective form of child-rearing that curtailed unruly or dangerous activities. Most critically, in her view, the street provided children with a perspective on the city and a sense of belonging to a larger community; it was "an unspecialized outdoor home base from which to play, to hang around in, and to help form their notions of the world."[12] Through this focus on the relationship between urban space and community, Jacobs added another layer to the criticism of existing playgrounds—making it more complex than just an attack on the design of play equipment—pointing to how they were disconnected from the street and thus the public life of the neighborhood. The work of Jacobs and other influential urban theorists from this period, including William "Holly" Whyte and Kevin Lynch, provided a framework for rethinking how the design of playgrounds and other public spaces could reflect and incorporate urban experience.[13]

Adventure Playgrounds

Dattner named Adventure Playground as an homage to the eponymous European playgrounds (initially known as junk playgrounds), which had gained notoriety during the early 1960s as the most radical alternative to the traditional playground. In 1943, Danish landscape architect Carl Theodor Sørensen created the first of these playgrounds in Emdrup, near Copenhagen. After observing that children seemed to prefer playing in construction sites and empty lots than in playgrounds, he decided to facilitate precisely this experience. He dedicated a space in which he provided children with tools and discarded materials and encouraged their inclinations to build and manipulate. Sørensen declared, "Of all of the things I have helped to realize, the junk playground is the ugliest; yet for me it is the best and most beautiful of all my works," elevating the play activity over notions of design and aesthetics.[14]

These playgrounds became popular in England, in London and other cities, following World War II through the efforts of British landscape architect and child welfare advocate Lady Allen of Hurtwood, who promoted them as an alternative to the new playgrounds resulting from postwar rebuilding and to address the disastrous effects of war on children.[15] Echoing the criticisms of American mothers, Hurtwood derided typical play equipment as "inflexible ironmongery."[16] She organized the creation of junk playgrounds on bombed sites, which children were already drawn to explore. By repurposing these ruins, children were seen as participating in the community's efforts toward renewal and reconstruction.[17]

As Hurtwood began creating these playgrounds in England, she realized the connotations of the word "junk"—that Sørensen had celebrated—were hurting her cause, so she changed their descriptor to "adventure" to emphasize the experience over the means.[18] "Adventure" was defined by a great variety of activities and both creation and destruction: building, dismantling, digging in the earth, making fires, gardening, and cooking. [**FIGS. 36 AND 37**] Children's efforts were supported by play leaders, who unlike those in earlier playgrounds did not organize activity, but merely facilitated and, as needed, assisted. The adventure playground was ultimately a flexible concept, predicated on the idea that children benefited from a richness of experiences and control over those experiences.[19]

New York's Parks Department was initially enthusiastic about the European adventure playgrounds; in addition to their promise of creative play, like vest pocket parks they were an alluring option for transforming the city's many empty lots.[20] But aside from a few isolated and community-initiated projects, the idea never took hold.[21] Instead, and somewhat ironically, the name "adventure playground" became synonymous with

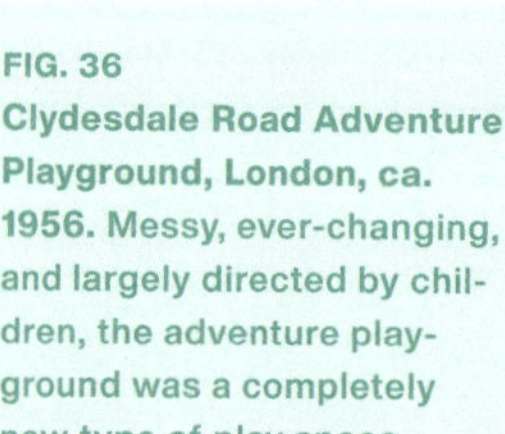
FIG. 36
Clydesdale Road Adventure Playground, London, ca. 1956. Messy, ever-changing, and largely directed by children, the adventure playground was a completely new type of play space.

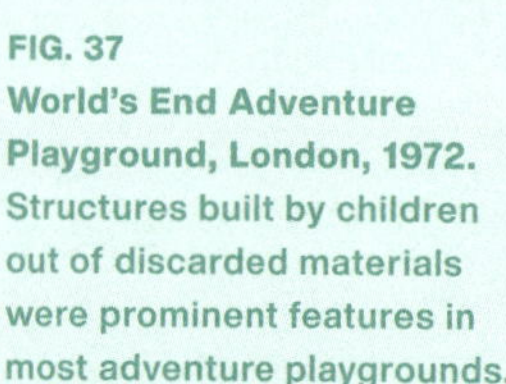
FIG. 37
World's End Adventure Playground, London, 1972. Structures built by children out of discarded materials were prominent features in most adventure playgrounds.

playgrounds designed by architects and landscape architects. (In contemporary accounts of these playgrounds, the word "adventure" was sometimes placed in quotes to denote this distinction.) Reflecting on the creation of Adventure Playground in Central Park, Leonard Lauder, who was aware of the European playgrounds, identified context as important: "What is appropriate for a bombed-out site in the heart of London is not appropriate for probably the greatest masterpiece of landscape architecture, which is Central Park and I would no more think of putting those bridges and tires and loose pieces of wood in Central Park than I would of putting in an elaborate structure in the middle of a bombed-out area."[22] Dattner noted that the chaotic appearance of the child-built playground was disconcerting to some parents, specifying that "middle-income parents don't like it because it looks messy and low-income parents don't like it because they think they're getting cheated."[23] Similar to play in the streets and ruins of postindustrial New York, the European adventure playground functioned primarily as a model—a revelation in the creativity of children. For a city in the throes of physical decline, it was not enough of a declaration of investment in urban space and children.

Dattner admitted that his interpretation—Adventure Playground in Central Park—was a compromise: "The next best thing to a playground designed entirely by children is a playground designed by an adult but incorporating the possibility to create their own places within it."[24] Nonetheless, he was intent on facilitating the experience of actual creation at the core of the adventure playground project. Early conceptual sketches show him working through this idea, illustrating children playing with what he called "adventure materials"—sticks, blocks, and panels that resembled oversized building toys.[25] [FIG. 38] He ultimately created modular, notched panels for children to build with and supplied other building materials, all of which were stored within an enclosure inside the playground's wood pyramid. [FIG. 39] Although most new playgrounds from this period did not involve play leaders, Adventure Playground was an exception: the community funded a full-time staff person to manage materials and provide assistance to children.

The Playgrounds of Isamu Noguchi

Dattner embarked on his first playground amid a controversy over a visionary playground design by artist Isamu Noguchi and architect Louis Kahn

FIG. 38
Richard Dattner, sketch of "adventure materials," 1967. Instead of junk, the architect envisioned modular forms that children could build with.

FIG. 39
Play panels, Adventure Playground, ca. 1967. Dattner ultimately created notched panels for use in the playground.

for a site in New York's Riverside Park. The project began in 1961 and its design evolved over the course of five years, with numerous changes to the plan driven by the conflict between the Parks Department, neighborhood residents, and the project's funders. For Dattner, the project provided not only a model for a designed form that could facilitate some of the experience of interaction and exploration inherent in street play and the adventure playground but an education in the breadth of political and cultural forces shaping the planning and design of playgrounds at this time.

Like most new playgrounds during this period, the Noguchi-Kahn playground was initiated by a group of mothers. After months of voicing concern about a dilapidated playground near West 103rd Street in the park, the mothers convinced the city to clean it up, add new play equipment, and reassign a playground director.[26] These successes inspired them to consider a more comprehensive renewal. Desirous of an innovative design and with an awareness of Noguchi's unconventional approach to playgrounds, the group sought his involvement.

Although he was best known as a sculptor, Noguchi's interest in playgrounds was a manifestation of his deep interest in the potential of art to shape the experience of everyday life, which also led him to pursue the design of gardens, fountains, lamps, and furniture. By the early 1960s, his playground designs had achieved mythic status, augmented by the fact that several were dismissed by Robert Moses, criticized as dangerous and unfeasible. The first rejected playground, *Play Mountain,* was conceived in 1933. Noguchi created a model of a monumental pyramidal form rising from an entire city block that incorporated slopes for sledding and sliding, a swimming pool, and a band shell for concerts. [FIG. 40] According to Noguchi, when he presented it to Moses in 1934, the newly appointed commissioner "laughed his head off and more or less threw us out."[27] As argued by scholar Shaina Larrivee, this reaction was less indicative of Moses's conservative design approach than of Noguchi's radicalism.[28] No artist had ever attempted to design a playground. Urban reformers had created the first playgrounds, approaching design as a utilitarian endeavor in service of their social agenda. When Noguchi walked into Moses's office, the Parks Department was just beginning the process of colonizing the city with playgrounds and codifying their design and program. Noguchi's vision of a playground as an earthwork (long before the earthworks movement of the 1960s) was incomprehensible to Moses and other park administrators.

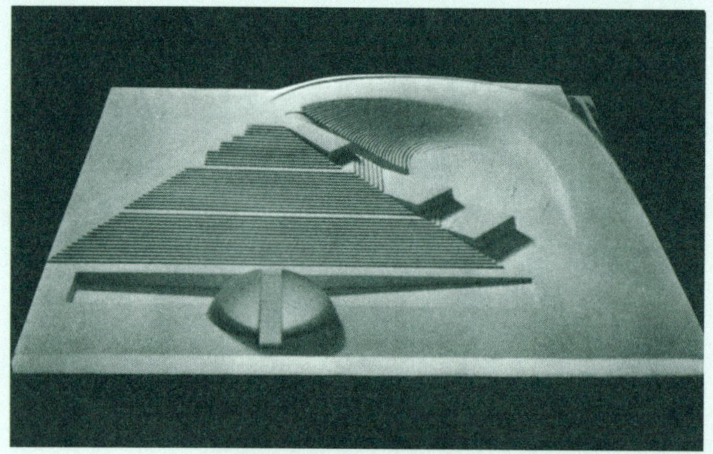

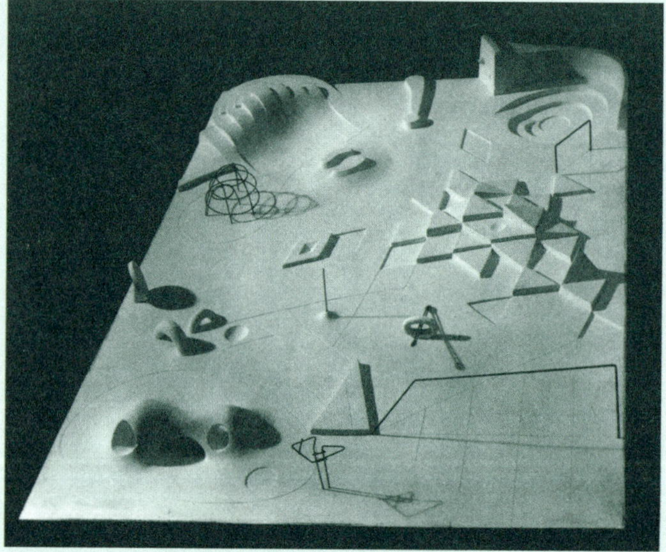

FIG. 40
Isamu Noguchi, model of *Play Mountain*, 1933. Plaster. Noguchi's first proposal for a playground was inspired by prehistoric architecture and earthworks.

FIG. 41
Isamu Noguchi, model for United Nations Playground, 1952. Plaster. Noguchi sculpted the ground plane into slides, mounds, a wading pool, and other forms, which were complemented by free-standing sculptures for play.

Moses went on to reject two subsequent proposals, including one for the United Nations in 1952 that illustrated Noguchi's continued experimentation with the relationship between geometric abstraction and play. [FIG. 41] Noguchi's only consolation was that the model was exhibited at the Museum of Modern Art, which generated excitement about his alternative conception of the playground within the arts community and beyond. The critic Thomas Hess, editor of *Art News,* attempted to envision the impact of this design on the play experience: "Instead of telling the child what to do (swing here, climb there) [the playground] becomes a place for endless exploration, of endless opportunity for changing play."[29] Noguchi was one of the first designers or artists to envision how the playground could be more than just a collection of equipment but a comprehensively designed environment with the potential to stimulate the child's imagination, a seminal idea that became the foundation of the work of designers such as Dattner and Friedberg. Reflecting on his legacy in 1975, Noguchi declared, "My ideas had never been tried. Now I see them everywhere."[30]

Embarking on the project in Riverside Park, Noguchi was hopeful about realizing his ideas about the relationship between abstract forms and creative play. Although he had reservations about working with the Parks Department, by the time the project started in 1961 Moses had left the agency, and his successor, Newbold Morris, had expressed enthusiasm. The project also had a donor, Noguchi's friend Audrey Hess (the wife of Thomas Hess), with whom he had worked on the United Nations playground. Furthermore, the community was invested, and ambitious. They wanted more than just a playground but a flexible, year-round space for all ages, including a nursery school and an amphitheater, which led the project to expand beyond its original concept and footprint.[31] The addition of buildings to the plan prompted Hess to invite architect Louis Kahn to collaborate with Noguchi, raising the profile of the project even higher. However, the Parks Department criticized their initial plans as grandiose and expensive, concluding the project would be an "unjustifiable architectural monument."[32]

Noguchi and Kahn revised their proposal to be smaller in scale and acreage, but they began to face a new obstacle: a group of neighborhood residents who were not involved in the initial planning became outraged over the destruction of parkland necessary to create such a large facility. Frederick Law Olmsted had designed Riverside Park with Calvert

FIG. 42
Isamu Noguchi, model for Riverside Drive playground, 1964. Painted plaster. This project, the culmination of Noguchi's vision of the playground as a sculptural landscape, had a great impact on the development of a new approach to playground design.

Vaux and Samuel Parsons Jr., and although it was a vastly different site than Central Park—a long, linear park along the Hudson River—it was similarly valued as an experience of landscape and retreat from the city. Neighborhood resident Barry Benepe called the Noguchi-Kahn plan "a violent interruption of the unbroken green banks forming the base of Riverside Drive."[33] A debate ensued between those who saw the recreational complex as an encroachment and those who saw it as a way to enliven underutilized park space and serve the community. Noguchi and Kahn released yet another plan in 1964, which they defended as sensitive to the landscape. The new design consisted of a unified arrangement of pyramidal and mounded forms complemented by shallow geometric forms that animated the ground plane. Kahn attempted to integrate the buildings into the existing topography of the site, making them less discernible as structures. [FIG. 42] Photographs of the model were featured in several design magazines and caught the attention of Dattner and others interested in new playground concepts.[34] However, persistent opposition and a resulting lawsuit continued to stall the project.

The fate of the Noguchi-Kahn playground was decided in 1966 during Mayor Lindsay's administration. Despite his and Commissioner Hoving's ardent interest in avant-garde playgrounds, they were reluctant to support the project because of their other goals for parks. Lindsay suggested that the playground would be more impactful in a neighborhood lacking recreational facilities, and Hoving opposed the project as an encroachment on historic parkland.[35] By April 1966, the lawsuit had made its way to the Supreme Court, which found that the project could not legally go forward because it had been bid out without sufficient funding in place to construct it.[36] Despite efforts to raise additional funds and discussions about adjusting the proposal to a new site, the project was abandoned.

In accounts of the history of this playground, scholars have expressed surprise and disappointment that such an extraordinary play environment designed by two luminaries was not unequivocally supported.[37] Yet the protestors' views of the playground as an encroachment was not anomalous, nor was it due to a lack of interest in modern design. The Battle of Central Park and other high-profile protests over proposals by Moses to radically alter public spaces and neighborhoods during the 1950s, along with the destruction of some of the city's significant historic buildings—most notably Pennsylvania Station—were the catalysts for the historic preservation movement in New York. This culminated in the city's creation of the Landmarks Preservation Commission in 1965, but despite the prominence of debates over public spaces, the agency regulated changes only to architecture.[38] The Noguchi-Kahn playground was one of many proposed additions to parks during the 1960s that prompted park users to demonstrate their value and the need for their protection. In response, Hoving promised to broaden the purview of the newly formed commission to include "land itself as a landmark."[39]

In his book *Design for Play,* Dattner reflected on the failure of the project and its deep impact on his approach to Adventure Playground: "In addition to its outstanding design, the doomed project yielded one very important lesson: the community must be fully involved in a project from its inception."[40] Dattner's response was an intensive program of community engagement, which consisted of numerous meetings with the mothers' group to develop the design, outreach to the broader community (including recent immigrants), presentations to children at local schools, tours of the construction site, and events in the playground to raise funds and garner support. This process was a priority for Dattner, and his detailed accounting of it in his book—intended as a guide for others—illustrates how citizen engagement was as critical as innovative design in developing a new approach to playgrounds. While Dattner's emphasis on this process may have been a response to the outcome of the Noguchi-Kahn playground, it also reflected the growing interest of landscape architects and other design professionals in generating new forms of community participation in the planning and design of the public realm.[41]

Play Sculptures

Noguchi's conception of the playground as a work of sculpture was so compelling to Dattner and others during the 1960s because it infused artistic values into a design practice primarily driven by functional concerns. The playground revolution was not only a response to widespread criticisms of playgrounds as unsafe and boring but also, in the words of one journalist, as "barbarically ugly."[42] During the 1950s, the development of alternatives to traditional play equipment—which reached a broader public than Noguchi's proposals—furthered both a new aesthetics of playground design and ideas about the relationship between design, play, and child development.

A toy company called Creative Playthings, formed in the 1940s, was the first to explore new directions in play-equipment design. The company initially became known for producing educational toys in collaboration with artists, characterized by their elemental forms and materials such as unpainted wood building blocks and trains or cars constructed of basic geometric shapes and with few details.[43] Desirous of bringing this vocabulary of abstraction to outdoor play, in 1953 it created a division called Play Sculptures, which sold manufactured designs by Noguchi, Swiss designer Antonio Vitali, and other well-known artists and designers. To promote this new venture, in 1954 the company sponsored a competition in conjunction with the Museum of Modern Art inviting artists and designers to propose sculptures for children's play. The museum exhibited the entries in a popular exhibition where visiting children were encouraged to try them. Consisting of modular abstract forms that could be arranged in a variety of ways,

FIG. 43
Play Sculptures in Carl Schurz Park, 1966. On the left is "Fantastic Village" by Virginia D'Orazio, the first-place winner of the Creative Playthings competition.

these novel play features aimed to create a bold visual statement while expanding the possibilities for play and exploration.

Beginning in the early 1960s, the Parks Department installed Play Sculptures and similar equipment by other manufacturers in playgrounds throughout the city—a shocking introduction of color and sculptural form. [FIG. 43] As scholar Amy Ogata has shown, Creative Playthings's embrace of abstraction was not solely an aesthetic direction; drawing from contemporary child psychology, the company promoted modern aesthetics as a means to inspire imaginative play. The company's marketing reflected and contributed to a larger discourse about creativity and the creative potential of the child, one that pervaded postwar, middle-class domestic culture.[44] To underscore the value of abstraction and its effect on creativity, some critics compared Play Sculptures to representational sculptures. One target was sculptor José de Creeft's *Alice in Wonderland* (1959) in Central Park. Consistent with other sculptures created for children in Central Park (and a favorite of Robert Moses), *Alice in Wonderland* embodied what many adults deemed appealing to children, primarily animals and storybook characters.[45] [FIG. 44] For those rebelling against traditional park design aesthetics, this realism

FIG. 44
Unveiling of *Alice in Wonderland*, May 7, 1959. Critiques of *Alice in Wonderland* as traditional ignored its immense popularity with children and modernist site design by landscape architect Hideo Sasaki. (Robert Moses is pictured on the right.)

was, like standardized play equipment, limiting. According to one critic, *Alice* was "too literal to stimulate the imagination."[46] Similar critiques were directed toward themed equipment based on animals, rocket ships, and cartoon characters, which also became popular during this period.[47] In contrast, Creative Playthings promised that the organic, open-ended abstraction of their Play Sculptures would inspire children to create their own narratives.

Although their effectiveness was later debated, Play Sculptures shaped parents' expectations of what the "creative" playground should look like. When the mothers' group advocating for a new playground in Central Park changed their name to the Committee for the Creative Playground (before Dattner became involved), they specifically requested Play Sculptures. These became widespread symbols of the new direction in playground design, and their popularity further elucidates why new playgrounds adhered to an aesthetic ideal rather than the programmatic concept of the European adventure playgrounds, despite the latter's more direct impact on a child's creativity.

The Playgrounds of M. Paul Friedberg

The landscape architect M. Paul Friedberg made wide-ranging contributions to the playground revolution, beginning with a series of projects that not only advanced innovative design concepts but proposed a completely new way of looking at play in the urban environment.[48] Jane Jacobs's critique of the disconnect between the recreational facility and the life of a neighborhood resonated with Friedberg. While Dattner's work in Central Park involved redesigning existing playgrounds, Friedberg's opportunities led him to dismiss the paradigm of the recreational facility all together and to design environments that encouraged recreational experiences and were integrated with their surroundings.

Friedberg developed this approach through projects that involved redesigning the open spaces within existing public housing developments. In the early 1960s, the federal government began pressuring the New York City Housing Authority (NYCHA) to innovate the design and management of its properties, most of which were urban renewal projects constructed during the 1940s and 1950s.[49] The layout of these developments consisted of high-rises that surrounded large lawns, which were fenced off from residents, with standard playgrounds located throughout. Emblematic of new pressures, lawns were becoming difficult to manage as residents defied the "Keep off the Grass" signs. The NYCHA began to work with landscape architects, architects, and artists to redesign these spaces for community use, typically with funding from philanthropists.[50]

In 1963, Friedberg collaborated with Pomerance and Brienes, Architects, to redesign the open spaces at the George Washington Carver Houses in East Harlem.[51] [FIG. 45] The Astor Foundation, a philanthropy dedicated to improving the lives of the poor, provided funding. Brooke Astor, the foundation's chairwoman, had chosen to support this particular project because she was "aroused by the sterile look of these spaces."[52] For this initial design, Friedberg broke from traditional park design, whereby space was divided into sections designated by function and age group and separated by paths and fences. Instead, he used changes in grade and walls, trellises, seating steps, and planters to parse the space into discrete

FIG. 45
Carver Houses Plaza, 1965. Friedberg designed the Carver Houses Plaza as a series of outdoor rooms that each invited multiple types of use.

but contiguous areas that accommodated a range of uses. The result was a dynamic urban plaza, a multipurpose space without distinct boundaries, which Friedberg hoped would afford residents agency over their recreational experience and inspire engagement with their environment and with one another.

Although Friedberg believed that the plaza was a success overall, he was dissatisfied with the section he designed for children, which included a wading pool, metal climbing bars, a series of concrete tubes (reminiscent of Play Sculptures), and sandboxes with concrete animal sculptures. [**FIG. 46**] Like Dattner, he was interested in learning from children at play and observed that they gravitated toward other parts of the plaza—running up and down steps and climbing a brick wall constructed in a pattern of protruding and recessed bricks, which functioned as foot- and hand-holds.[53] [**FIG. 47**] The space he had designed specifically for children's play failed to engage them because it consisted of, in Friedberg's words,

FIG. 46
Playground at Carver Houses, 1965. Although the playground was more integrated into its surroundings and included some customized features, like traditional playgrounds it was composed of isolated elements.

FIG. 47
Wall at Carver Houses, 1965. Friedberg did not design the wall for climbing, but children appropriated it as a play feature.

"static pieces, offering static experiences," a criticism that pointed to the limitations of Play Sculptures.[54] It did not promote the exploration of space and form that Friedberg observed happening in the rest of the plaza.

For Friedberg's next project, at the Jacob Riis Houses on the Lower East Side, he attempted to design a playground driven by his concept of the urban plaza as a multifunctional and integrated space. As at the Carver Houses, he incorporated the playground into a rhythmic series of spaces comprising sitting areas, a fountain, and an amphitheater. However, the playground was completely unprecedented. When the plaza opened in May 1966, many did not know what to make of the playground; one journalist described it as a having the "mystery of a primitive city discovered after lost eons."[55] [FIG. 48] Its most prominent features were pyramidal and mounded forms in different sizes reminiscent of those proposed by Noguchi for Riverside Park. Perhaps inspired by the wall at the Carver Houses plaza, Friedberg made the forms climbable by facing them with granite

FIG. 48
Riis Plaza playground, 1966. Friedberg realized the first example of a playground as unified, topographically varied landscape for play.

block. He further expanded the possibilities for interaction by inserting tunnels through the forms and installing slides on their surfaces. Configurations of wooden blocks connected the forms on the ground and arched metal ladders spanned them higher up. [FIGS. 49 AND 50] These connections between and through features solved the problem of static and isolated elements: Children could climb up a pyramid and then slide down it, climb on stepping forms to a nearby mound, enter a tunnel leading to an internal ladder, climb up to the top and over to the next form on another ladder, and so forth. He called this fluid exploration "linked play."

In addition to introducing topography to the playground, Friedberg incorporated new materials and utilized traditional ones in new ways. Constructed of granite, concrete, wood, metal, sand, and water, the playground had a pronounced materiality that Friedberg hoped would encourage children to experience "the richness and excitement of color; the emotional responses to light and dark; the sensuality of textures—rough, smooth, soft, gritty; . . . the range of the auditory sensation including echo,

FIG. 49
Ruth Orkin, Riis Plaza playground, ca. 1966. Key to the experience of this space were connections between play features, which promoted what Friedberg called "linked play."

FIG. 50
Ruth Orkin, Riis Plaza playground, ca. 1966. Friedberg's concept of linked play appears to have inspired linked children.

FIG. 51
Barton Silverman, Lady Bird Johnson with residents of Riis Houses at the opening ceremonies for Riis Plaza, May 23, 1966. Riis Plaza inspired great hope in the potential of urban design and innovative playgrounds to improve the lives of children in low-income neighborhoods.

cacophony, melody and resonance."[56] Presenting children with a variety of textures, colors, and forms promoted a deeply sensual engagement with the play environment, and this epitomized how these playgrounds deviated from earlier models. The adults involved in earlier playgrounds aspired to the ideals of character-building, exercise, and (sometimes) pleasure, which they saw as universally beneficial to children. Friedberg sought to recognize the child's agency in play and design the playground as a source of individual experience.

The design of Riis Plaza received much critical attention, becoming a model for urban designers and park administrators, and the playground—its most acclaimed feature—was a direct influence on Dattner's design for Adventure Playground.[57] Created for a predominately low-income, minority community, it signaled that innovative playgrounds were not the privilege of well-off city residents nor primarily to address the problem of the white middle-class fleeing to the suburbs. For critics of urban renewal, this dramatic transformation of underutilized open space represented a redemptive paradigm for public housing that prioritized the needs and well-being of residents. Indicative of the prominence of this project, then-president Lyndon B. Johnson's wife, Lady Bird Johnson, delivered the dedication address on May 23, 1966, and afterward wrote to Brooke Astor, whose foundation had funded the plaza, that it was proof that the country was "moving ahead" and "may be the lifeline that saves someone or creates someone."[58] [FIG. 51] Architecture critic Ada Louise Huxtable was full of praise, predicting that the project would "set national standards ranging from the simple pursuit of 'beautification' to the solution by design of some of the American city's pressing social problems."[59] These aspirations recall those of the reformers at the turn of the twentieth century who invented the playground in response to the societal upheaval caused by urbanization. Sixty years later, amid a new urban crisis, politicians, designers, and philanthropists had revived the playground as a vehicle for social reform.

3

The Adventure-Style Playgrounds of Central Park

In the twelve years following the creation of Adventure Playground, the Parks Department administered projects in nine of Central Park's existing twenty-two playgrounds, five of which were designed by Richard Dattner. While appearing in varied configurations that incorporated the ongoing development of ideas about design for play, the playgrounds continued to be defined by sculptural, interconnected forms and by the prominence of interactive materials, such as water and sand. Building on the earliest examples, Riis Plaza playground and Adventure Playground, supporters of new playgrounds still promoted them as part of a larger process of urban revitalization, which was evident also in the landscapes of Central Park. Amid intense questioning of the city's viability and concerns over its future, the park emerged as the premier stage for discussions about and demonstrations of the value of recreation and public space. Central Park is also a place to explore how the playground revolution ended, beginning with a gravitation away from custom, site-constructed environments back to manufactured play equipment and, finally, when the city's interest shifted away from playgrounds, to the park itself.

Central Park's collection of adventure-style playgrounds illustrate how a broad public network became involved in the design and use of open space during this period. Reacting to the top-down approaches to planning and design epitomized by the Moses administration, the Parks Department endeavored to be more responsive to the needs and interests of citizens and established a Community Relations Division to better facilitate outreach and communication. When mothers living in almost all of the neighborhoods bordering Central Park wrote to the city demanding upgrades to playgrounds—enumerating skinned knees, bored children, and broken benches as evidence of the need for change—the Parks Department dutifully responded to all of the letters but with regret.[1] As the city attempted to realize its ambitious plans for playgrounds and parks, it was stymied by lack of funds.[2] To make up for budget shortfalls and to fund expensive projects, Hoving, whose mission was "to make it chic for the wealthy to give money to the city's parks rather than buying third-rate Renoirs," actively cultivated private funding for new projects, targeting philanthropies and corporations. In response to those mothers demanding overhauls to Central Park's playgrounds, he encouraged them to raise the money themselves.[3] Hoving also broke from the traditional in-house design process, hiring designers from private firms, sometimes high-profile ones, to infuse new vision into the agency and attract sponsors.[4] Employing Adventure Playground as a model for public-private partnership, citizens living in the blocks neighboring the park initiated and, in most cases, also funded new playgrounds. The role of the Parks Department was as a networker—connecting parents with designers and donors—and as a project manager, overseeing the design and construction process.

Other forms of citizen activism and engagement were evident in Central Park during the late 1960s. In 1966, after the city changed a rule banning political rallies in the park, it became the site of numerous demonstrations against the Vietnam War, indicative of how the Parks Department endeavored to make the park open to new forms of cultural and political expression. Park landscapes themselves were frequently the source of protest, with numerous proposals to introduce new structures leading to fierce public debates about the park's value and purpose. The motivations of protestors defending the park against additions were consistent with those in the past—like the mothers engaged in the Battle of Central Park, they were concerned about the destruction of landscape and intrusions on its scenic beauty and experience. But the activism during this period was fueled by new urgencies and interests. Concern about the park's deteriorating condition, a growing awareness of its history and significance—the Secretary of the Interior had designated the park as a National Historic Landmark in 1965—and the citywide historic preservation movement all propelled the more vehement resistance to change in the park.

Commissioner Hoving and subsequent administrators were instrumental in calling attention to the park's history and design. Influenced by his previous career as a curator at the Metropolitan Museum of Art and his study of Olmsted while a student at Princeton, Hoving sought to revive the idea of the park as a work of art. Declaring that the park "need[ed] to be cared for as an artistic entity," Hoving vowed to fight against additions and appointed a curator, architectural historian Henry Hope Reed, to promote the park's history, advise on historic preservation projects, and evaluate proposed changes.[5]

As new, decidedly modern additions, the adventure-style playgrounds appeared inconsistent with the administration's purported focus on protecting and preserving the park. During the planning for Adventure Playground, Hoving declared that "building in Central Park is not something I am in favor of."[6] Yet new playgrounds were not entirely new: They involved rebuilding the existing playgrounds that had been installed during the Moses administration. Commissioner August Heckscher (Hoving's successor) explained, "Whatever harm the park suffered as a result of the addition of these playgrounds had occurred long since."[7] The Moses administration's installation of playgrounds along the park's perimeter created a framework that made possible the proliferation of adventure-style playgrounds. Tucked away in liminal landscapes and ensconced within a rigid footprint, the playgrounds could be modernized without infringing further on the park's design and purpose.

The park during this period was defined by other new forms of urban play—a variety of events and programs, which the Parks Department promoted similarly to playgrounds as a way to enliven the park without significant impact. While Hoving celebrated the park as a work of art that needed careful study and specialized care, he also recast it as an exuberant stage, declaring, "If you leave it sitting, nothing is going to happen."[8] Central Park hosted more and larger events than ever before, as well as different types: numerous popular music concerts, art festivals, and innovative programs known as happenings. As in the past, the Sheep Meadow was the primary venue, but instead of folk-dancing festivals for children, it hosted a midnight party to watch meteor showers, a Barbra Streisand concert, and a "Be-In," a gathering of youth instructed by organizers to "Come as you are."[9] [FIG. 52] These highly publicized events drew the public back into a place they had largely been avoiding. One of Hoving's most transformative schemes was to close the park's main roads to vehicles on Sundays in order to encourage biking and walking, which like events facilitated new forms of park experience and community.

The proliferation of events in Central Park was part of a broader mission to envision the entire city as a stage and thus engender a vibrant and inclusive cultural scene. Lindsay merged the city's Office of Cultural Affairs with the Parks Department, creating the Parks, Recreation, and

FIG. 52
Barbara Streisand concert on the Sheep Meadow, 1967. The concert was the largest gathering for a performance in Central Park's history.

Cultural Affairs Administration (PRCA), which focused on expanding the scope and geography of the arts by appropriating streets and parks in neighborhoods throughout the city as the sites for programs, performances, and art works.[10] During 1967, the Metropolitan Opera performed for free in several neighborhood parks; the Public Theater staged performances of Shakespeare in Central Park; artists painted murals in parks and playgrounds; and "mobile units," traveling entertainment centers, brought movies, dance, fashion shows, music, and theater to neighborhoods throughout the city.[11] [FIGS. 53 AND 54] Epitomizing the PRCA's attitude toward integrating the arts into the fabric and life of the city, Commissioner Heckscher described *Sculpture in Environment,* the city's first large-scale exhibit of public sculpture, as a way to "let these great pieces loose in the city and to set them under the light of day where they intrude on upon our daily walks and errands."[12] This focus was as practical as political: compared to ambitious schemes for rebuilding parks, the administration could implement arts programs with minimal planning and funding. (Like playgrounds, most programs were privately funded.) Arts programming reanimated the public realm, signaling that

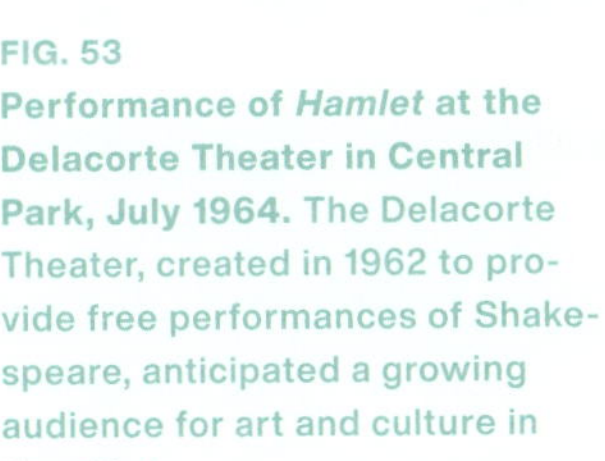

FIG. 53
Performance of *Hamlet* at the Delacorte Theater in Central Park, July 1964. The Delacorte Theater, created in 1962 to provide free performances of Shakespeare, anticipated a growing audience for art and culture in New York.

FIG. 54
Mobile unit production of *Flying Sun Power,* 163rd Street in the Bronx, August 1968. The portable entertainment facilities known as "mobile units" were the result of the Parks Department's mission to offer expanded recreational opportunities in underserved neighborhoods.

New York was still a "fun city," as Lindsay had declared, despite mounting social and economic issues.[13]

Playgrounds as Community Development

The project that followed Adventure Playground was a smaller intervention that did not receive nearly as much critical attention yet was further revealing of the process of community involvement in playground rebuilding and its relationship to other forms of urban revitalization. At the end of 1965, Robert and Kim Weintraub, Upper West Side residents and parents of three young children, approached the Parks Department about making improvements to the dilapidated playground located near West 81st Street, across the street from their apartment building. Motivated by a desire to fix up their neighborhood, they began with Central Park, which they considered their front yard.[14] They donated funds for a spiral slide and several Play Sculptures, as well as rubber safety mats and tire swings, all of which they specifically requested.[15] [**FIG. 55**] To make more of a mark, they hired Richard Dattner to create a water feature and worked with him on developing the design. Dattner, who was inspired by the myriad ways children played with water in the street, had realized that providing a multifaceted experience of water was central to the creative playground project. [**FIG. 56**] The playground opened in September 1967 with the water feature as its focal point. [**FIG. 57**] It comprised four concrete towers of different heights, each containing a nozzle that children could adjust and that emitted water with varying intensity, ranging from a fine mist to a stream-like flow. The water poured into adjacent wading pools, which provided another site for and type of water play.

The *New York Times* described the project as just the beginning of a "one family urban renewal thrust," which would involve additional efforts to "make the neighborhood more livable and pleasing to the eye."[16] The family's impetus of neighborhood improvement and the *Times*'s use of "urban renewal" in a positive context made the small project emblematic of a shift in approaches to urban redevelopment. Jane Jacobs's attack on urban renewal as the wholesale removal of historic neighborhoods and public opposition to similarly destructive highway construction projects during the 1960s had galvanized grassroots efforts to protect and revitalize neighborhoods that focused on rehabilitation and enhancement.[17] The descriptions of the project also revealed how because Central Park's playgrounds were

FIG. 55
West 81st Street Playground, opened in 1967. The installation of a spiral slide manufactured by Creative Playthings was part of the initial effort to revitalize the existing Moses-era playground.

FIG. 56
Katrina Thomas, West 114th St., in Harlem, 1968. Children playing with water in the street provided Dattner with the inspiration for an interactive water feature for the West 81st Street Playground.

FIG. 57
West 81st Street Playground, 1967. The water feature could also be used for climbing, exploring, and games when the water was turned off.

FIG. 58
Public School 166 Playground, 1969. The Board of Education and the Parks Department created this playground for both school and broader neighborhood use with funding from the Astor Foundation.

located close to park entrances and were such significant centers of community life, efforts to update them were considered as much a form of neighborhood as one of park improvement.

A growing number of adventure-style playgrounds on the Upper West Side contributed to the neighborhood's revival, specifically by making it more attractive to families. By the late 1960s the neighborhood, long associated with a high crime rate and a varied but decaying housing stock, was experiencing a turnaround, evidenced by new housing developments cropping up on empty lots, families returning from the suburbs to renovate brownstones, the opening of new businesses, and new playgrounds.[18] In addition to the West 81st Street Playground and Adventure Playground (which *New York Magazine* reported in 1969 was becoming overcrowded), M. Paul Friedberg designed two playgrounds in the neighborhood: one for the courtyard of Columbus Park Towers, a small subsidized housing development on West 94th Street and the other for the schoolyard at Public School 166 on

FIG. 59
Courtyard at the Stephen Wise Towers, ca. 1965. The courtyard's central feature was a grouping of eighteen cast stone horses, which the sculptor Constantino Nivola intended for children's play.

West 89th Street. [FIG. 58] Another contribution to this collection was the courtyard of the Stephen Wise Towers, a public housing development on West 88th Street.[19] Completed in 1964 as part of the New York City Housing Authority's efforts to enliven its open spaces, it featured murals, fountains, and sculptures by the artist Constantino Nivola. [FIG. 59] Inspired by the success of their first playground, the Weintraubs began planning to update the playground at their children's public school on West 77th Street. Although this project did not materialize, their impetus reflected the growing momentum around playgrounds as catalysts of neighborhood change.

Further north, on the fringes of the Upper West Side, a group of parents took community involvement in playgrounds to another level by not only initiating but also designing a new playground for Central Park. The project began in 1967, when mothers formed Parents for Improved Playgrounds to advocate for the creation of an "adventure playground" to replace the dilapidated playground at West 100th Street.[20] The mothers had visited Adventure Playground, which provided their initial inspiration, and even consulted with the Committee for a Creative Playground. Their impression of the Parks Department as somewhat ineffectual led them to decide that "the best course of action would be to completely redo the

FIG. 60
Esther Ross of Parents for Improved Playgrounds with her children at the opening of Discovery Play Park, 1973. Like most playgrounds of this period, the project was initiated and shepherded by mothers.

playground ourselves."[21] Marilyn Ryan, one of these mothers, remembers sitting in the playground with friends and realizing that many of their husbands worked in design fields. They encouraged the fathers—industrial designer Jim Ryan and architects William Jacquette and Kenneth Ross—to form a partnership to design the playground.[22] Although Marilyn Ryan also remembers thinking they were "too far uptown to matter," in a neighborhood that was more racially and economically diverse than the others bordering the park, the group's advocacy ultimately attracted the attention of the Lauder Foundation, which agreed to fund its construction.[23] After six years of planning and design, the playground opened in 1973. For Commissioner Heckscher, the playground was a model collaboration—"a fine example of the city, the community and private sources working together for a neighborhood and for park improvement."[24] [FIG. 60]

Continuing this legacy of family involvement, Julia Jacquette, the daughter of architect William Jacquette, wrote and illustrated a graphic memoir, *Playground of My Mind* (2017), about her experience of this and other playgrounds of this era.[25] (Jacquette grew up in Columbus Park Towers where she played in the Friedberg-designed playground.) The book provides a rare child's perspective on these spaces and how they resonated into adulthood. The designers of Discovery Play Park had absorbed the lessons of the playground revolution, particularly the ideal of an integrated

FIG. 61
Illustrative Plan of Discovery Play Park by Ryan, Ross, & Jacquette Architectural Associates, 1973. A central bridge divided the playground into an area for older children (top) and one for younger children (bottom).

play environment with an abundance of play opportunities for children of different ages. [FIG. 61] Jacquette remembers the astonishing variety of things to do, many of which involved risk-taking and imaginative play: swinging on "Tarzan ropes" from a raised wooden platform, climbing up the "volcano" and sliding down, and traversing a rope bridge from one tree house to another. [FIGS. 62 AND 63] She also remembers that the "interconnectivity of everything was thrilling," conducive to a deep exploration of form and space. [FIG. 64] The play experience provided an education in design—a sense of composition and vocabulary, which allowed her to make connections to other designed spaces throughout the city, and this ultimately informed her decision to become an artist. Jacquette's reflections and the story of the playground's creation illuminate how the social and civic impact of these playgrounds was ideally all-encompassing, reaching the child, family, and community and extending into the park, neighborhood, and city.

FIG. 62
Julia Jacquette and her brother in Discovery Play Park, 1973. The playground included custom climbing structures constructed in wood.

FIG. 63
Julia Jacquette in Discovery Play Park, 1973. The "volcano" in Discovery Play Park was reminiscent of mounds in other adventure-style playgrounds but was distinguished by red ceramic tiles on its surface and a roller slide, which offered a more tactile sliding experience.

FIG. 64
Discovery Play Park, 1973. The playground was densely packed, with many of the play features physically linked to one another.

Historic Preservation and Modern Design in Central Park

The playground revolution coincided with the historic preservation movement and both shared origins in the growing demands of citizens for greater involvement in decisions about public space. Both frequently intersected in Central Park, a commingling of the somewhat conflicting impulses to update the park while also protecting it. In a couple of instances, adventure-style playgrounds were the direct result of park encroachments, presented to the public as concessions for the appropriation or destruction of parkland. Aside from revealing the inadvertent ways some of these playgrounds came into being, these projects illustrate the singular position in Central Park of adventure-style playgrounds, which were acclaimed as contemporary additions and examples of modern design at a time of widespread resistance to both.

The expansion of the Metropolitan Museum of Art during the 1970s ultimately resulted in the creation of one of Dattner's most well-known playgrounds—Ancient Play Garden (now known as Ancient Playground), which opened in 1973. Hoving, who had left the Parks Department to become the director of the museum in March 1967, led the expansion project, which was part of a master plan conceived for the museum's 1969–70 centennial. Initial phases included the expansion of the American Wing and a new extension, the Lehman Wing, both of which would subsume landscapes on the west side of the museum and face the park with huge glass walls.[26] Planning also began for a glass pavilion on the north side of the museum to house the Temple of Dendur, an Egyptian antiquity, which became the catalyst for changes to two existing playgrounds in this area. The temple was to arrive in August 1968—in over six hundred crates—long before the museum could build a permanent home for it; in the meantime, the museum endeavored to create a storage and staging area. According to Hoving, the only site for this was the small playground directly adjacent to the museum. Although Commissioner Heckscher was incensed by this idea—he did not support the museum's plans, seeing them as the ultimate encroachment—he ultimately agreed to Hoving's concession to create a new "museum-oriented playground" on the site, to be designed by Dattner and constructed with funding from the Lauder Foundation.[27] Soon after, in a separate turn of events, a group of Upper East Side mothers began advocating for improvements to this and another playground about a block north, a larger space with a restroom. The mothers, who had formed the

Committee for the Improvement of the 84th Street Playgrounds, learned of the museum's plans and met with Dattner to discuss. They proposed a new plan: to redirect the effort and funds to the larger and more popular playground and to eventually restore the other playground as a landscape.[28] This was ultimately the direction taken.

Despite the attraction of another innovative playground and Hoving's promise that "anything we build will be, in some manner, a sympathetic extension of the park," the museum's plans were fiercely controversial.[29] Protestors opposed the overall expansion, with one declaring, "The duplicity of the museum is that it pretends to rescue nineteenth century art but ignores Central Park, the city's greatest example of such art."[30] They also focused on the specific location and architectural character of the plans. Architecture critic Ada Louise Huxtable, one of the most outspoken advocates for the park during this period, noted that the landscapes surrounding the museum had over time become particularly crowded. With the two playgrounds, the museum's parking lot, an ancient Egyptian obelisk, baseball fields, and the Shakespeare theater, the area was "an obstacle course of existing encroachments."[31] While Huxtable acknowledged that many of these additions were well-used and appreciated, collectively they represented a manifestation of Olmsted and Vaux's greatest fear—that the park would become, in Olmsted's words, a "desultory collocation of miscellaneous amusements," at the expense of open space, landscape, and a retreat from the city.[32]

The museum's expansion, designed by the firm of Kevin Roche and John G. Dinkeloo, proposed the introduction of modern materials and forms into the park, which also incited debate. An earlier proposal for a café in the southeast corner of the park had been influential in cementing general attitudes about additions, as well as raising the question of whether modernist architecture was appropriate in any form. Initiated in 1960 by a gift of $500,000 from the millionaire Huntington Hartford, heir to the A&P supermarket fortune, the proposed café was a two-story pavilion with sliding glass walls designed by Edward Durell Stone.[33] [FIG. 65] The building appeared foreign and obtrusive in the rocky terrain near the water body known as the Pond, relegating the landscape to a mere backdrop—the complete inversion of Olmsted and Vaux's approach to architecture as secondary to landscape. Further diminishing the status of this landscape, project supporters asserted that the area would benefit from the café

FIG. 65
Model of the Huntington Hartford Café designed by Edward Durell Stone, 1962. The proposed café was met with vehement opposition from citizens and civic organizations.

FIG. 66
Lasker Pool and Rink, ca. 1965. The combined pool and skating rink was the largest and the last recreational facility built in Central Park.

because it was "neglected and misused."[34] The project was immediately met with resistance, with the *New York Times* proclaiming in an editorial: "We are against any more invasions into Central Park, so beloved by the public that it has become something special, something almost sacred."[35] After years of protests and a lawsuit, the city abandoned the project. Modernism did make its way into the park in the form of the Lasker Pool and Skating Rink designed by Fordyce and Hamby, which opened in 1966 in the northern end of the park, at the edge of the large swath of woodlands that defined the wild and rustic character of the area. [FIG. 66] This project, which was initiated in 1958, did not incite any protest, likely because of its somewhat remote location. However, Huxtable derided the addition as an

FIG. 67
Existing playground at East 85th Street, ca. 1972. Totally disconnected from the park by roads, this site was ideal for a modern intervention.

"artistic anachronism" and "like a jazzed-up concrete bunker in a sylvan setting," highlighting the disconnect between modernist architecture and picturesque landscape.[36]

The Parks Department and the community wholeheartedly embraced new playgrounds because they had minimal impact on the park. The site for Ancient Play Garden, the museum-inspired playground, was a traffic island created by the entrances to the transverse road; with its entrance on Fifth Avenue, it was more connected to the neighborhood. [FIG. 67] Dattner developed the design with input from the mothers' group and in consideration of the proximity to the museum and the new addition to its Egyptian collection. Returning to the archetypal forms that had informed his first playground, Dattner designed play features inspired by ancient Egyptian architecture, including an obelisk, pyramidal forms, a sundial, and a water feature inspired by the Nile River, all of which he hoped children would connect to artifacts found in the museum.[37] [FIGS. 68–70] According to the Parks Department, this was the first historically themed playground, introducing a didactic dimension to the playground revolution.[38] It is unclear if children took note of these references to ancient history, which were somewhat veiled in abstraction, and the robustly architectural design bore little resemblance to a garden. The overall effect of the playground's varied topography, the density of forms, and the rich palette of materials was that of an intricate obstacle course; the playground further defined "adventure play" as vigorous physical exploration, an endless loop

FIG. 68
Illustrative design for Ancient Play Garden, 1972.

FIG. 69
Water feature in Ancient Play Garden, ca. 1973. From its source in the obelisk (left), the water flowed into an elevated channel and then cascaded into the wading pool, demarcated by bollards that sprayed water.

FIG. 70
Ancient Play Garden, 1973. Dattner surfaced play features with dark brown brick, a reference to the use of this material by ancient Egyptians.

FIG. 71
Heckscher Playground, 1969.
The portion of Heckscher Playground redesigned by Dattner contained features becoming familiar as part of his repertoire: interconnected tree houses and a climbing mound with tunnels and slides.

of sliding, scrambling, and climbing. With its towering wood climbers and brick-faced pyramids, the playground also resembled a city, but one that looked nothing like its urban context and this distinctness reinforced the paradigm of the playground as a self-contained child's world.

Dattner's final and most ambitious playground in Central Park was also born of the tumultuous advancement of external forces into its landscapes. In 1969, Dattner redesigned a section of Heckscher Playground, the park's largest and oldest playground. [FIG. 71] Soon after it opened, the Parks Department learned that the Metropolitan Transit Authority (MTA) was planning to construct a subway tunnel connecting Manhattan and Queens, which would necessitate trenching through the southeastern corner of the park. The new playground was directly in its path. Commissioner Heckscher lamented, "If the subway planners had wanted to strike a blow to the heart, they could not have aimed it more nicely!"[39]

Civic groups and park advocates began protesting immediately, most vehemently about the destruction of trees and rock outcrops. After an extended negotiation between the MTA and the Parks Department, the MTA shifted the tunnel's location, reduced the amount of digging, and agreed to restore all affected landscapes.[40] In addition to rebuilding the playground slated for destruction, they promised to fund another intervention by Dattner in a different section of Heckscher Playground. However, the lack of planning and coordination had created mistrust in city government, and despite these promises, the start of construction was met by protestors, mostly mothers and their children. In a scene that recalled the Battle of Central Park, they tried to physically obstruct the work.[41]

The tunnel debacle created an opportunity for Dattner, resulting in the culmination of his experiments with water and his only site-specific design. Constructing it in the previous location of a wading pool, Dattner used the existing infrastructure to create what he called the Water Playground. When it opened in June 1973, just in time for summer, the *New York Times* heralded it as the "newest concept in 'adventure' playgrounds," and described soaking wet children marveling at how water was everywhere.[42] The playground comprised granite-faced climbing mounds linked to one another by elevated channels and to the ground by ladders, slides, and poles. [FIG. 72] Sprinklers installed within the elevated sections flooded these channels, and the water flowed into a ground-level area with a series of wading pools and a concrete and metal climbing structure that sprayed more water. [FIG. 73] One child exclaimed, "I never saw a jungle gym with water coming out of it before."[43] Dattner extolled the multi-sensual properties of water and its potentials for play: "It moves, it's infinitely malleable, it's cool in the summer, it makes a pleasant sound . . . and it's just nice to look at."[44]

Dattner, who has expressed fascination with the park's geology, designed the water feature so that it emerged from the massive rock outcrop that formed its backdrop, creating the impression that water was flowing from the rock and making an unprecedented link between playground and park. [FIG. 74] This intervention contrasted the natural with the manmade, the historic with the modern, but afforded a fluid experience from one to the other, employing Friedberg's idea of linked play in a new way that was particularly salient in this location. Heckscher Playground was the site of the park's first designated area for children and later the first playground, reshaped again by Dattner according to the latest ideas about urban play. Surrounded by ancient rock and the park's relatively unaltered

FIG. 72
The Water Playground, 1973.
Dattner integrated spray features, streams, and wading pools into a sprawling stone-and-concrete structure.

FIG. 73
The Water Playground, 1973.
Although Dattner focused on water play, he also designed the playground for use when the water was turned off.

FIG. 74
The Water Playground, 1974. Children, who typically entered the park's playgrounds through an iron gate, could climb from the rock directly into the water feature.

landscapes, it was a manifestation of how ideas about play and recreation had changed over time.

Play beyond the Playgrounds

In 1974, a playground designed by Dattner located near East 72nd Street in Central Park was the setting for a dance performance, an event that intimated an expanded scope and meaning of urban play during this period.[45] Appearing in the classic television special *Free to Be You and Me,* a multiracial group of young men and women performed "Brothers and Sisters," a spirited song and dance that promoted the message of inclusiveness and gender equality that was the theme of the program. The performance showcased the playground, with its multiple levels and interconnected forms, as an ideal stage for dance. [FIG. 75] The performers jump on and off cylindrical concrete forms, twirl and swing on tire swings, dance along the playground's low concrete walls, and somersault from a slide into the sand that formed the surface of the playground. In the playground context

FIG. 75
East 72nd Street Playground, ca. 1970.

FIG. 76
East 72nd Street Playground, ca. 1970. A maze-like configuration of low walls provided structure to the design and demarcated the various play areas, while also providing seating for spectators.

FIG. 77
Adventure Playground, 1967. Steps and low walls were a common feature in adventure-style playgrounds.

and through the performers' interactions with play features, the choreographed dance became a form of play. Alternatively, the design of this and other adventure-style playgrounds, with play features and small plazas surrounded by low walls intended as seating or steps, afforded parents and children a front row seat for the performance of play.[46] [FIGS. 76 AND 77]

This blurring of the lines between art and play was also evident beyond the playground fence. Commissioner Hoving's approach to the park itself as a stage made it fertile ground for new ideas about urban play, ideas that were most vividly expressed in events called "happenings." Distinguished from a traditional event or performance by the participation of the audience, the origins of the happening lay in ideas about the dematerialization of art that had been percolating in the art world since the late 1950s. The artist Allan Kaprow first used the term to describe experimental performances typically initiated by a set of instructions or guidelines and enacted by spectators or other participants, ideally resulting in spontaneous actions and chance incidents. If art was not an object but an experience, as Kaprow declared, it could happen anywhere. He identified "old lofts, basements, vacant stores, natural surroundings, and the street" as potential settings.[47] In his many writings, Kaprow espoused a philosophy of art as a form of ludic experience; the happening was "a game, an adventure, a number of activities engaged in by participants for the sake of playing."[48] By the mid-1960s, the idea of the happening had entered popular consciousness, and the term was used to denote a variety of gatherings or events presented as hip and interactive. For Hoving, the happening served as a model for expanding the locations for art and culture, and moreover, for participatory events that invited a deeper engagement in place and community.[49]

In May 1966, the Parks Department staged *Cartoon Performance*, the first happening in Central Park, installing a 105-foot-long canvas on a grassy slope known as Cedar Hill and inviting the public to paint on it.[50] [FIGS. 78 AND 79] The Parks Department had facilitated many arts programs in the past, but these were typically small-scale, highly organized activities targeted toward children. *Cartoon Performance* was an unprecedented experiment to invite the public to make art in a park setting. The lack of structure and instructions—participants were free to paint whatever they desired—was also a vehement break from convention. The experimental artist Phyllis Yampolsky, whom Hoving had appointed as "artist-in-

FIG. 78
***Cartoon Performance,* 1966.** The first happening in Central Park was both an arts program and a public spectacle.

FIG. 79
Commissioner Hoving's contribution to *Cartoon Performance,* 1966. Hoving, who often participated in happenings, offered this homage to Olmsted.

FIG. 80
Scene from *Build-Your-Own-Castle-and _______*In-It Day,* 1966. The only site-specific happening in Central Park was inspired by the park's own castle, seen on the distant hill.

residence" and who was well-versed in the improvisatory ideal of the happening, helped conceive of and organize the event. She later organized other happenings, also known as "experimental public games," which all evinced a dynamic between individual creative exploration and community gathering and celebration. For *Build-Your-Own-Castle-and_____*In-It Day* in Central Park, she organized an activity reminiscent of the European adventure playgrounds, providing participants with art and building materials and encouraging them to create structures inspired by Belvedere Castle, one of the park's most iconic buildings. [FIG. 80] The blank and asterisk in the title encapsulated the spirit of the happening—the open-endedness and unpredictability that was a potential source of personal expression.

The Parks Department organized *Cartoon Performance* in conjunction with an exhibit called *The Object in the Open Air* at the Museum of Contemporary Crafts (now the Museum of Arts and Design), which documented how ideas of participatory play permeated the art and design of this period and made explicit connections between happenings and new playgrounds. The museum's director explained that collectively the exhibit and the happening were intended to showcase "new ideas and new concepts in playground living."[51] Through the provocative use of "playground" as an adjective, the word transcended its definition as a purpose-built space, becoming a state of being that was activated by designed form or (loosely) programmed activity. The exhibit juxtaposed models for public sculpture, documentation of happenings, and photographs of the most illustrious examples of postwar landscape architecture, including the town of Reston, Virginia, a planned community; Lawrence Halprin's design for Lovejoy Plaza, the first park in his famed Open Space Sequence in Portland, Oregon; and Friedberg's playgrounds. Predicated on the idea that design should not proscribe use but create opportunities for choice and exploration, these spaces shared with one another—and with happenings—a dual purpose as sites of aesthetic engagement and stages for social interaction.

In addition to public programs, art festivals in Central Park demonstrated the shifting and intersecting definitions of art and play, while exposing the limits of the park as a cultural stage. The Fourth Annual New York Avant Garde Festival in September 1966 was the first in Central Park and unprecedented as a presentation of contemporary art in a public space.[52] The experimental musician and performance artist Charlotte

FIG. 81
Allan Kaprow's happening *Towers,* 1966. The artist instructed participants to roll tires down a hill and aim to knock over wooden posts draped with plastic, fabric, and tin foil. At the felling of each post, a horn blasted.

FIG. 82
Balloon dome, 1966. It is unclear whether or not the balloon dome was a work of art.

Moorman organized the festival, which featured close to one hundred works in a variety of media, including installations, music performances, poetry readings, and happenings, many taking place simultaneously. Moorman had staged previous festivals in a concert hall; with the park as venue, she aimed to reach a broader audience, a goal that corresponded with Mayor Lindsay's aspirations for a more inclusive cultural scene. Moorman explained, "I am very bored with the concept that art is for few people, the chosen few. . . . I have a secret love for reaching people who don't get to museums or concerts normally. . . . I'm very interested in fun and not making art such a snobbish, mysterious thing."[53] Some installations, such as a dome filled with balloons, and Allan Kaprow's happening *Towers,* explicitly combined art and play and were particularly alluring to children, making them part of the expanded audience for art. [**FIGS. 81 AND 82**]

Although the event was celebrated in the art world, it was not as enthusiastically embraced by some park devotees. The festival took place in the area known as Conservatory Water, which epitomized a Moses-era vision of park recreation—and of public art. Its main features were a small pond, popular for model boating, and two beloved sculptures, *Alice and Wonderland* and *Hans Christian Anderson,* the latter the site of a regular storytelling program for children. Festival performances such as Bici

Hendricks's *Washing Event,* consisting of washing diapers in the pond, and Al Hansen's *Three Events,* which involved stringing toilet paper in trees, angered some visitors and advocates. The park curator, Henry Hope Reed, called the festival a "desecration," the utmost affront to the park as "one of the finest examples of public art."[54] An editorial in the *New York Times* acknowledged the exceptional social impact of events such as these but questioned the sacrifice—the loss of tranquility, the disruption of landscape scenery—and urged that "the emphasis on 'happenings' not be permitted to subvert the less spectacular values that a park affords."[55] Similar to the proposed additions, the reconceptualization of Central Park as a stage for "playground living" brought the park itself into greater relief, inspiring proclamations of its original purpose as an urban oasis and its value as a work of art in its own right, ultimately reasserting the park as central to discussions about the role of recreation in urban life.

New playgrounds, happenings, and art festivals resulted from the dissolution of the boundaries that had defined ideas about and spaces for urban recreation and art in the past. Friedberg's philosophy that "recreation is not a fenced-off part of our lives, just as education does not occur only in a school" corresponded to Kaprow's belief that "the line between art and life should be kept as fluid, and perhaps indistinct, as possible."[56] Removing these boundaries uncovered play as more complex than a physical activity, a way to fill leisure time, or a source of a child's education and development, which were the traditional functions of play in a recreational context. Cultural historian Johan Huizinga formulated an expanded definition of play in his influential book *Homo Ludens* (1950), which Kaprow and Dattner both had read. The book provides a framework for understanding the prominence of play in 1960s art and culture. Huizinga posited that while play has numerous extrinsic benefits, it is not a means to an end. The true purpose of play, what actually motivates and benefits the player, is the experience of play—characterized by the "fun-element" [*sic*] and a state of intense immersion in the play activity. In pinpointing this fundamental purpose of play, he provided a new reading of cultural history. By arguing that play is not limited to the sphere of childhood but pervades all forms of culture, including literature, philosophy, even law, he magnified play as "one of the main bases of civilization."[57] In the parks, playgrounds, and streets of 1960s New York, and in a concentrated form in Central Park, play was a generator of culture, innovation, and community—elevated into an art form and as a vehicle for urban revitalization.

The Playground Revolution and Manufactured Play Equipment

Cultural programs that appealed to a wide audience were ultimately more far-reaching than adventure-style playgrounds. The ideal of the playground as a unique environment, tailored to the needs of the community, was difficult to realize comprehensively. Referring to Dattner's playgrounds in Central Park, one Parks Department administrator admitted, "You obviously are not going to be able to dot the city with these things."[58] In a period of declining resources such customized environments were simply too expensive to build and too labor-intensive to program and maintain. The city built approximately forty new play environments between 1966 and 1980 (including vest pocket parks and Central Park playgrounds), the majority of which were completely privately funded.[59] Their concentration in Central Park was due in large part to the sustained advocacy of neighborhood mothers who had the time, financial resources, and even political acumen to invest in these projects. Although Hoving and other playground advocates eschewed manufactured equipment because of its associations with standardization and banality, it became the means to a more widespread transformation of playgrounds and the focus of the next, and last, phase of the playground revolution.

Manufactured equipment made primarily of wood became popular in the early 1970s and was installed in playgrounds throughout New York and nationwide through the 1980s. Aside from its popularity, wood equipment is important to this history as the direct result of Friedberg's relentless experimentation and determination to make the playground revolution more accessible and impactful. The evolution from idea to unique design feature to manufactured equipment was an unplanned, organic trajectory. Friedberg had used modular wood elements to develop his idea of linked play at the Riis Plaza playground, creating stepping forms and bridges that were critical to achieving the experience of the playground as a totality. He continued to experiment with modularity with wood after receiving a grant in 1966 from the Department of Housing and Urban Development to create designs for vest pocket parks. Friedberg conceived of four systems consisting of prefabricated forms, in wood and other materials, which could

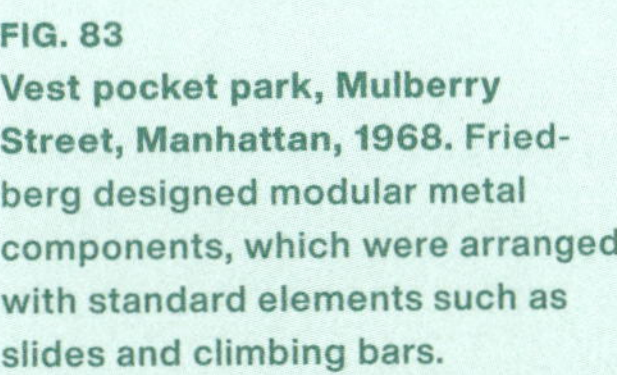

FIG. 83
Vest pocket park, Mulberry Street, Manhattan, 1968. Friedberg designed modular metal components, which were arranged with standard elements such as slides and climbing bars.

FIG. 84
Vest pocket park on Pacific Street in Brooklyn, 1968. A flexible and affordable material, wood was ideal for vest pocket parks.

FIG. 85
Playground at Pruitt-Igoe, St. Louis, ca. 1969. Created when Pruitt-Igoe was becoming severely deteriorated and as many residents were leaving, the playground seems to have been an attempt at investing in the remaining community. The complex was completely demolished by 1976.

be arranged innumerable ways. In 1968, the Parks Department installed ten of these play systems in empty lots throughout the city.[60] [FIGS. 83 AND 84]

Designers and park administrators in other cities soon became interested in using wood in playgrounds.[61] Around 1968, the managers of Pruitt-Igoe—the notorious housing development in St. Louis that by the late 1960s had become a symbol of the failure of urban renewal—approached Friedberg about building a wood playground there. Friedberg's interest in modularity extended beyond his goal of a flexible and affordable design concept; he saw it as a vehicle for creative expression and even social cohesion.[62] For Pruitt-Igoe, he provided wood posts of varying lengths, some with carved details, which he intended for the community to assemble without a specific design or his intervention on site. [FIG. 85] Ideally the process of building the playground from this "kit" would be a step toward community rebuilding.

Soon after the project at Pruitt-Igoe, Friedberg began working with his supplier, a lumber brokerage called Neidermeyer-Martin, to explore marketing and selling these kits, which he still envisioned that parks

FIG. 86
Friedberg working on designs for TimberForm with designer Sonja Johannson, 1968.

FIG. 87
TimberForm installed in a playground in Kansas City, ca. 1975. TimberForm and other manufactured wood equipment became the new standard in urban playgrounds but could be arranged in various ways that made each playground unique.

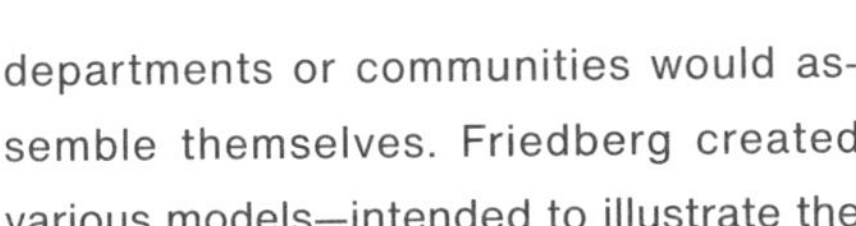

departments or communities would assemble themselves. Friedberg created various models—intended to illustrate the possibilities—but it was these fixed designs in which customers expressed interest. ("The creative instinct wasn't as strong as I thought it was," Friedberg reflected later.)[63] Working with Neidermeyer-Martin, he further codified designs for play features—configurations of stacked timbers called "Play Stacks," as well as stepping forms, arch climbers, and tire swings. [FIG. 86] They called the product TimberForm and agreed that Friedberg would receive a commission on sales. The product line was ultimately acquired by the company Columbia Cascade, which became the country's leading supplier of wood play equipment.[64] [FIG. 87]

In Central Park, all the playgrounds designed by Dattner included wood equipment, features that are not so well known as integral to these spaces because most of them did not endure. [FIG. 88] In the late 1970s, three Central Park playgrounds were rebuilt almost entirely with wood. [FIG. 89] The most elaborate was Spector Playground at West 86th

FIG. 88
Tire Swings, East 72nd Street Playground, ca. 1970. Dattner's playgrounds included tire swings, climbers, and tree houses constructed in wood.

FIG. 89
The East 96th Street Playground, built in 1979. Wood equipment such as these TimberForm models was far more ubiquitous than the concrete features that are typically associated with the playground design of this era.

FIG. 90
Spector Playground, opened 1976. This playground included a combination of manufactured wood equipment, custom features built in wood, and a concrete water feature.

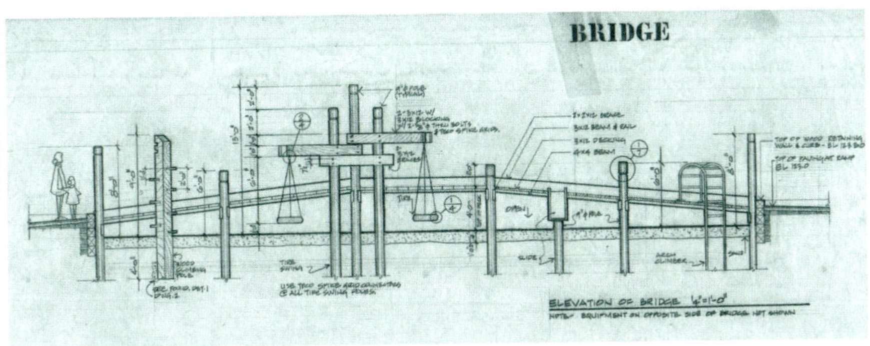

FIG. 91
Bridge at Spector Playground, 1976. This central feature, which recalled the bridge at Discovery Play Park, incorporated tire swings and various apparatus for climbing.

Street, designed by Abraham Rothenberg, an architect who lived on the Upper West Side, and constructed with funds raised by the Community Playground Association, a neighborhood group.[65] The playground's great variety of features—tire swings, tree houses, bridges, climbers, a pyramid, and a pergola—demonstrated the potential of wood to advance the goal of the playground revolution to enrich possibilities for play. [FIGS. 90 AND 91] This and other wood playgrounds had a handcrafted aesthetic that evoked Friedberg's original do-it-yourself ideal: features constructed out of standard planks and poles resembled popular building toys, and the custom constructions recalled the child-built structures in the European adventure playgrounds, especially as they aged.

The Parks Department installed other types of manufactured equipment in the city's playgrounds during the 1970s, much of it in response to Creative Plaything's Play Sculpture line. [FIG. 92] While sculptural play equipment had generated excitement about the potential for reinvigorating the design of play equipment, Friedberg and others found its play value limited. Lady Allen of Hurtwood, the promoter of adventure playgrounds, derided it as "over-slick" and "immobile."[66] Ada Louise Huxtable asserted that it appealed more to adults than children, calling it "an adult conceit . . . that foists a pretentiously false estheticism on those too young to protest."[67] New models appeared to be influenced by Friedberg's ideas about linked play, illustrating an evolution from individual sculptural object to play systems combining various modular units. In Central Park, the Parks Department installed "Magic Forest," manufactured by the

FIG. 92
Play Sculpture in a Brooklyn schoolyard, 1966. Many installations of Play Sculptures consisted of isolated objects.

FIG. 93
Magic Forest in the East 76th Street Playground, ca. 1980. Similar to Friedberg's modular designs, the variety and interconnectedness of forms were intended to provide a more dynamic play experience.

Playground Corporation of America, in the existing playground located at East 79th Street. [**FIG. 93**] The company marketed the ensemble of various concrete and metal units as a vehicle for imaginative exploration, describing it as a "captivating environment of abstracted trees, stumps, branches, platforms and shadowy places."[68]

Dattner contributed to this offshoot of the playground revolution with a product called PlayCubes, which was installed in Central Park and other city parks in 1969. Expanding on his ideas for "adventure materials" first explored during the planning for Adventure Playground, he designed a modular system of individual cuboctahedrons (a polyhedron with eight triangular faces and six square faces) made of fiberglass and pierced with holes, which could be bolted together to create clusters for climbing and exploring.[69] [**FIG. 94**] Park administrators praised PlayCubes and other modular designs for their affordability and ease of installation—similarly to the happenings and other cultural programs, they could transform an empty lot or a park lawn into a site for play.

From Playgrounds to Park

Although events, programs, and playgrounds succeeded in drawing the public back into the park, which in turn spurred a reawakening to the park's value, they failed in the Parks Department's other mission—to protect it.

FIG. 94
PlayCubes designed by Richard Dattner in Central Park, ca. 1969. The Parks Department called these installations "Instant Playgrounds."

Poor management of events and lack of general maintenance resulted in the severe degradation of the park's landscapes and infrastructure. A *New York Times* article from 1974 described the scene: "Much of the grass is worn away. The ground is packed hard as concrete. The trees are dying, and the duck pond is a bed of mud and crumbling rock. It is overused, trampled upon, neglected, disrespected and abused."[70] [**FIGS. 95 AND 96**]

The celebration of Olmsted's 150th birthday on April 30, 1972, was a last hurrah of sorts epitomizing the uneasy coexistence of interests that characterized this period in the park's history. The event featured a huge cake in the shape of and decorated as the park, an Olmsted impersonator, and performances by the all-city high school chorus and the experimental theater group Theater for the New City. The event reflected the growing appreciation and awareness of Olmsted, whom commissioners Hoving and Heckscher had been instrumental in promoting and whose accomplishments were becoming more widely known through exhibits and other scholarship.[71] Some in attendance at his birthday party made a connection between the event and the recent celebrations of Earth Day

FIG. 95
Eroded hillside, Central Park, ca. 1975. Landscape erosion was one of the park's most serious problems, a result of trampling and deteriorated drainage infrastructure.

FIG. 96
Shoreline of the Pond, Central Park, ca. 1975. Landscape erosion contributed to the deterioration of paths and the siltation of water bodies.

on April 22. Supporters of the environmental movement had also sparked interest in Olmsted, presenting his advocacy for large urban parks and approach to designing in concert with nature as relevant to the ecological consciousness of the mid-twentieth century.[72] However, the most "green" activity occurring on Olmsted's birthday was a "Free Pot!" parade, promoting the legalization of marijuana. Commissioner Heckscher recalled the event in his memoir, concluding, "The people ate the park."[73]

As the era of the "fun city" was coming to a close, the city and the public's focus on Central Park was beginning to shift away from events and playgrounds to address the realities of the park as a living, historic landscape in the throes of severe decline. Some park advocates had been trying unsuccessfully to initiate this shift for years, using the adventure-style playgrounds as an example of the Parks Department's misdirected and contradictory focus. To one outspoken critic of park policies, Robert Makla, the park was "the greatest adventure playground created," and instead of new playgrounds, it needed "enlightened restoration of its natural resources."[74] Park curator Henry Hope Reed had pointed out that the cost of Adventure Playground greatly exceeded the entire annual budget of $30,000 for planting in all Manhattan parks.[75] These two advocates founded the Friends of Central Park in 1965 to further their cause, and in 1973 the group organized and funded two small historic preservation projects that served as an object lesson for a new approach to the park: the reconstruction of a series of wooden shelters that had been installed along the shoreline of the central water body known as the Lake in the 1860s and the renovation of the Ladies Pavilion, a small cast-iron structure designed by Vaux.[76] [FIGS. 97–99] Another prominent project of this type was the renovation of Bow Bridge, one of the park's most iconic features, funded by philanthropists Lucy G. Moses and Lila Acheson Wallace. Designed by Vaux as one of the thirty-six bridges and arches that formed a key part of the park's circulation system, in 1972 when the project was initiated, the bridge was on the verge of collapse, its cast-iron structure rusting and wood decking rotting. The *New Yorker* reported that bridge looked like it had been mugged.[77] Building on the citizen investment in the park's playgrounds, these projects were notable as the earliest efforts to restore the park's original features.

In September 1973, the city announced a plan to rescue the park—a ten-year program of work, estimated to cost $55 million, resulting in

FIG. 97
Shoreline of the Lake with boat landing, Central Park, ca. 1973. The reconstruction of long-lost, historic features provided a small portal into the nineteenth-century park.

its comprehensive restoration.[78] Momentum continued to build when, in 1974, the city designated Central Park a Scenic Landmark, the first designed landscape to be given this status in New York.[79] The Landmarks Preservation Commission began to regulate any additions or changes to its design—a victory for park advocates and their sustained fight against encroachments. Advocates hoped the designation would pressure the city to begin work, but the city's fiscal crisis, which peaked in 1975, thwarted any further action. Parks—upheld as a vital urban resource during the Lindsay administration—were increasingly neglected as the meager city budget was allocated to fund more "essential" services.

The fiscal crisis also marked the end of the playground revolution. The approach of Parks Commissioner Edwin Weisel (appointed in 1973) was to "just hold together what we have, instead of building more playgrounds we have nobody to maintain."[80] Attrition and layoffs of staff, slashing of budgets, and administrative chaos—including six different

FIG. 98
Jack Manning, assembling the Ladies' Pavilion in Central Park, September 12, 1973. The renovation of the Ladies' Pavilion, which was almost destroyed by vandalism and lack of maintenance, was another example of the shift in attention to the park's historic design.

FIG. 99
Ladies' Pavilion, ca. 1973. The newly restored Ladies' Pavilion stood out against the littered and degraded landscape that surrounded it.

parks commissioners between 1973 and 1978—decimated the Parks Department.[81] In 1977, most of the city's playgrounds were not staffed and were cleaned only once a week, and many of the adventure-style playgrounds fell into disrepair.

As the condition of the park reached a nadir, the harsh reality of a dwindling Parks Department inspired more vigorous citizen-led efforts to address its condition and discussions about alternative approaches to its management. In 1974, a group of citizens formed the Central Park Community Fund, which focused on raising funds for maintenance projects and equipment.[82] The group also commissioned a study of the park by Columbia professor E. S. Savas. This first comprehensive analysis of the park since the 1920s examined its use, condition, and management. It identified mismanagement as a primary cause of the park's condition, noting specifically that the organizational structure of the Parks Department was not conducive to managing Central Park or other large parks effectively. The study concluded that what the park needed most was centralized oversight and clear policies governing park use, and it recommended a single administrator supported by a board of citizen guardians to manage the park.

These recommendations were grounded in a recognition of Central Park as extraordinary and unique, both as a recreational amenity and pioneering work of landscape architecture and as critical to the vitality and culture of New York. To address the realities of intense use, restore its intricate design, and rebuild its antiquated infrastructure would require a significant allocation of resources and an innovative approach to management. Debate over the park's governance continued until the end of the decade, including one proposal for the National Park Service to take control of the park, culminating when in February 1979 the city decided to create a centralized office within the Parks Department to manage Central Park and appointed Elizabeth Barlow as the administrator. The following year, she helped to initiate the Central Park Conservancy. Modeled in part after the city's cultural institutions and following the recommendations of the report by Savas, it consisted of a board of directors tasked with fundraising for the park's restoration and advising the work of the Office of Central Park Administrator.

Ushering in this new era was a project to restore the Sheep Meadow, which the concerts, demonstrations, and happenings of the

1960s and 1970s had reduced to a dustbowl. The project returned the meadow to a lush expanse of lawn, a literal erasure of the recent past and vehement embrace of the original vision for the park as a scenic landscape and urban oasis, which would guide the work of the conservancy in the coming decade.

4

Preservation and Stewardship of Adventure-Style Playgrounds

As the Central Park Conservancy was beginning to rebuild the park, an opportunity arose to consider how to incorporate playgrounds into this effort. In 1981, the Robert Wood Johnson Charitable Trust donated funds to create a new playground in memory of a family member, Billy, who had died in a motorcycle accident. The conservancy announced a competition to redesign the existing playground near East 67th Street, inspired by the park's landscapes. The conservancy's idea to "relate to the landscape outside [the playground's] perimeter," was a dramatic break from the paradigm of the playground as a contained, inward-focused space that corresponded to the organization's mission to comprehensively restore the landscape experience envisioned by Olmsted and Vaux while lessening the impact of later additions.[1]

M. Paul Friedberg submitted the winning design, which used stone, wood, water, and plants to create a literal microcosm of its surrounding—and was an homage to Olmsted and Vaux.[2] In a conceptual plan, Friedberg articulated his intent to create a connection between landscape and play: "Create a play environment without perceived equipment—the natural environment creates its own context for play: Climbing, Exploring, Etc."[3] [FIG. 100] The completed playground comprised a granite slide, rustic wood structures, a naturalistic wading pool, and numerous plantings, all directly inspired by the design and experience of the surrounding landscapes. [FIGS. 101 AND 102] Wood posts of varying heights bordered paths and planted areas, providing structure to the design while also functioning as a play element. [FIG. 103] While this rustic playground looked nothing like Friedberg's earlier, emphatically architectonic playgrounds, it was still based on his concept of linked play and belief that a playground should relate to its context. For the first time in Central Park, a playground appeared as a part of the park, not distinct from it.

Billy Johnson Playground opened in 1987 amid a period of transition for playgrounds in New York, one that was defined by growing

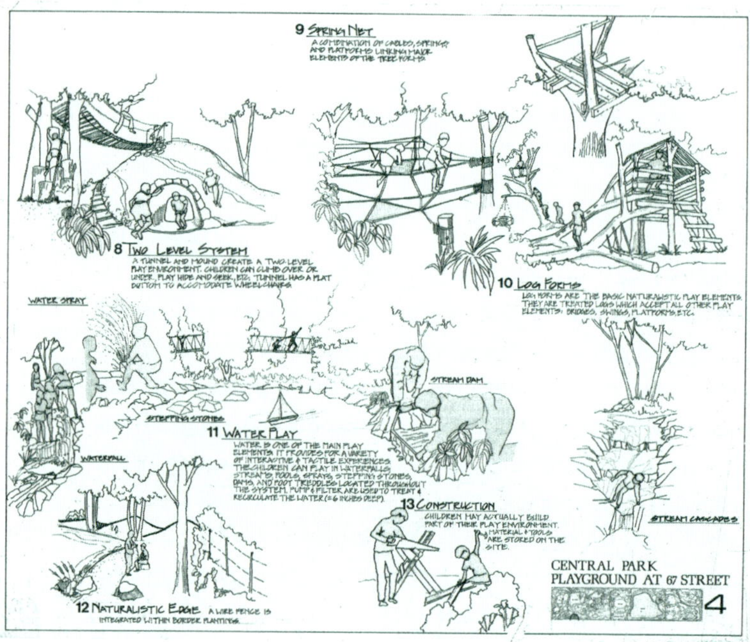

FIG. 100
M. Paul Friedberg, conceptual plan for Billy Johnson Playground, 1981. Friedberg envisioned a Central Park–inspired playground as a series of nature play experiences.

awareness about playground safety, a changing culture of childhood, and particularly the city's efforts to rebuild public spaces in the aftermath of the fiscal crisis. The state of the city's park system in the early 1980s was bleak; it was no longer in the decline of the 1950s, but in ruins.[4] A survey conducted in 1986 revealed that many playgrounds, particularly those in poor neighborhoods, suffered from deterioration and lack of maintenance—epitomized by broken equipment, shuttered restrooms, clogged sprinklers—and were marred by graffiti and trash.[5] During the 1980s and 1990s, the city made significant progress, repairing broken infrastructure and amenities and installing equipment whose design reflected new guidelines for playground safety. In this next chapter of playground history, the Parks Department focused on providing safe, clean, and functional spaces—ideally reviving the playground's role as a vital node of community life.

The conservancy's approach to playgrounds during this period was consistent with that of the city. While Billy Johnson Playground was

FIG. 101
Billy Johnson Playground, 1987. The stone bridge spanning a naturalistic wading pool evoked Gapstow Bridge at the nearby 59th Street Pond.

FIG. 102
Billy Johnson Playground, 1987. Friedberg designed a granite slide integrated into the slope of a hill to recreate the experience of sliding down rock outcrops.

FIG. 103
Billy Johnson Playground, 1987. Inspired by the rustic wood structure overlooking the playground and other similar structures throughout the park, Friedberg made wood a primary material in the playground.

FIG. 104
Slide in the West 85th Street Playground, 1980. By the early 1980s, the remaining Moses-era playgrounds were almost fifty years old and severely deteriorated.

a promising model for a playground integrated with the park that artfully fused the ideals of the past with the new ambitions for Central Park, it was a site-specific design that was challenging and expensive to realize.[6] During the 1980s and 1990s, the conservancy installed new equipment and performed upgrades in each of the playgrounds untouched during the playground revolution. [FIG. 104] These projects were opportunistic, initiated by the availability of funding (typically from private donations) or implemented as part of larger projects to rebuild different sections of the park. A master plan for the park, *Rebuilding Central Park: A Management and Restoration Plan,* published in 1985, demonstrated the conservancy's priorities. The plan was based on three years of work by a team of landscape architects and consultants, and while it examined many aspects of the park in detail, including use, vegetation, and infrastructure, and outlined specific plans for park areas, it did not comprehensively address playgrounds.[7]

Amid these efforts to rebuild the city's parks, the adventure-style playgrounds began to resurface. By the early 1990s, some had been removed out of concerns about their safety, and those that remained had become severely deteriorated. When the conservancy began planning a project to update Adventure Playground, proposing to replace some of its signature features, a group of community members launched an effort to preserve it. This appreciation of playground as artifact challenged the longstanding notion of the playground as a functional space subject to cyclical change. What followed was the development of an approach to updating the playground that sought to balance preservation and change, and ultimately a new era for the adventure-style playgrounds in Central Park.

Playground Safety and the Changing Landscape of Play in New York

Safety had been a perennial concern of designers, advocates, and park administrators ever since the invention of the playground, but it became a more pronounced issue beginning in the 1970s.[8] Earlier efforts to improve safety, such as the installation of rubber matting in the 1960s, were responses to injuries but were limited by a lack of comprehensive information. This changed in 1972 with the Consumer Product Safety Commission's (CPSC) creation of the National Electronic Injury Survey System (NEISS) to collect data on the safety of various consumer products. The NEISS collected information on playground injuries from a sampling of hospital emergency rooms nationwide, which led to a greater understanding of how they were occurring and what equipment was posing hazards. (For example, the survey determined that most injuries were caused by falls onto hard surfaces.) The data and research formed the basis for the CPSC's guidelines for the design and maintenance of public playgrounds, which the organization published in 1981 and has updated periodically ever since. Further studies of playground safety and the need for more technical information led the American Society for Testing and Materials to produce standards for playground surfacing in 1988 and play equipment in 1993.

The guidelines and standards compelled play equipment manufacturers to update their designs to respond to safety recommendations—or risk liability for injuries.[9] Simultaneously, advancements in manufacturing technology facilitated more complex designs in plastic, metal, and rubber, as well as a greater range of colors.[10] Manufacturers that had been working primarily in wood began producing play systems in brightly colored metal and plastic, known as "superstructures" or post-and-platform equipment. Consisting of a series of decks linked by bridges, attached to which were steps, slides, ladders, and poles, the design of this equipment derived from that of the earlier wood equipment, and ultimately Friedberg's concept of linked play. [FIG. 105] Manufacturers marketed this new equipment as more durable, easier to maintain, and certified as compliant with standards.

The first comprehensive modernization of New York playgrounds since the 1930s inspired mixed reactions.[11] Mothers and park administrators from the 1960s derided the Moses-era equipment as uninspiring,

FIG. 105
Post-and-platform play equipment at the West 96th Street Playground, installed 1992.

unsafe, and too pervasive, but as the city systematically removed traditional equipment such as slides and seesaws, replacing them with new post-and-platform systems, some parents (by this time fathers had become involved in playground issues) lamented the loss of these vestiges of their youth. Community members also commented, with one "dismayed to see the monkey bars and what they represent destroyed, only to be replaced with the ubiquitous playground equipment you see everywhere."[12] Moving beyond nostalgia, others worried that the new equipment did not provide enough opportunity for risk-taking and creative play. Henry Stern, who as parks commissioner from 1983 to 1990 and again from 1994 to 2000 oversaw much of this transition, admitted that safety standards had resulted in "blander equipment" than in the past.[13]

The city's removal of sandboxes revealed how this period was informed by broader attitudes toward the urban environment. Sandboxes were difficult to keep clean, and the Parks Department, still understaffed, did not have the workforce necessary to maintain them. Publicized reports of sandboxes harboring animal feces and drug paraphernalia made them unpopular, and many parents perceived them as unsanitary.[14] Richard Dattner commented, "The sandbox has become a microcosm of the city, harboring needles and other recent urban ills."[15] The removal of sandboxes occurred alongside efforts to address other urban ills, such as those to eradicate graffiti and other examples of vandalism and to police low-level crimes such as public drinking and panhandling. During the late 1980s, the city began to initiate renovation projects in parks to deter uses that hindered their broader access. Examples include Bryant Park, where drug dealing and prostitution were rampant, and Tompkins Square Park, much of which had become a homeless encampment. Influenced by the "broken windows theory," these initiatives were predicated on the belief that the physical transformation of the urban environment would influence public order, better facilitate its regulation, and perpetuate collective engagement and stewardship.[16] Guiding the management of Central Park was the conservancy's belief that "a dirty, littered park encourages careless, inconsiderate behavior on the part of its visitors. Good routine maintenance and consistent public education builds respect for the park."[17] New playgrounds, with colorful equipment that was certified as safe, were part of this investment in and vision for public space.[18]

These prevailing attitudes influenced perceptions of the adventure-style playgrounds, many of which were removed during this period. Riis Plaza, which in the 1960s had been widely regarded as a masterpiece of urban design, was demolished in the late 1990s with no apparent acknowledgment of its celebrated history.[19] According to the New York City Housing Authority (NYCHA), the plaza's intimate spaces, defined by walls and trellises, created hiding places and hangouts for drug dealers and users. Prior to its demolition, the space had been gradually altered: NYCHA installed fences—which Friedberg had so vehemently denounced—to regulate access and replaced the playground's mounds with standard equipment. Friedberg defended his design, asserting that lack of maintenance resulting in an unkempt appearance had made the plaza conducive to antisocial activities. In 1985, Brooke Astor, whose foundation had funded the plaza, expressed disappointment in its condition, noting the graffiti and litter, symbols of lost hope. "What I had envisioned has not come to be," she lamented.[20]

The investments in playgrounds during the 1960s and 1970s evinced their central role in urban life and childhood, which had been unwavering since their beginnings. The subsequent changes to playgrounds, characterized by a focus on safety, were also a manifestation of their diminishing status within the culture of childhood.[21] Beginning in the 1970s, many middle-class parents began enrolling their children in organized sports and after-school programs, a restructuring of free time that aimed to better prepare children for future success.[22] At-home entertainments, such as television, video games, and the proliferation of new types of toys, also usurped children's time that had previously been spent in playgrounds. In schools, time for recess on the playground was increasingly reduced to free up time for test preparation. While still a prominent feature in the urban landscape and a symbol of the city's health, playgrounds were no longer the primary space for children's recreation.

Playgrounds and Historic Preservation

In 1990 a group of parents approached the conservancy about the condition of Adventure Playground, expressing the prevailing concerns about safety and functionality. They saw numerous issues: the water feature was broken, the tunnel inside the climber was filled with trash, the gravel surfacing was slippery, the wood pyramid was rotting, and the concrete was a safety hazard.[23] The conservancy hosted a series of meetings with parents resulting in consensus that the playground was outdated and that a more comprehensive overhaul was preferable to piecemeal repairs. Three options were discussed: demolish the entire playground and create a new one, remove the elements considered hazards and replace them with new equipment, or replace the pyramid (the most severely deteriorated feature) and make targeted repairs and alterations to improve safety throughout.[24] Most parents expressed interest in the second option, in part because many of them liked the existing water feature. Adjacent to Adventure Playground was a renovated playground that likely provided a model for this approach. This was the playground created in 1956 as the concession to mothers following the Battle of Central Park, which had had been redesigned in 1969 by Dattner. [FIG. 106] Known as the Lower Playground (a reference to its spatial relationship to Adventure Playground), by the 1980s it was dilapidated, and another parents' group initiated the renovation out of concern that it had become a "hotel for homeless people."[25] [FIG. 107]

In 1995, the conservancy began planning the project in Adventure Playground as part of its second major fundraising campaign, focused on the park's west side landscapes. It confirmed the scope of the project as targeted repairs and upgrades throughout the playground, including

FIG. 106
Lower Playground, 1969. Dattner's design was a small intervention targeted to young children.

FIG. 107
Lower Playground following renovation, 1989. There was no apparent outcry over removal of Dattner's design, nor about the West 81st Street Playground, which the conservancy updated also in 1989.

replacing deteriorated wood features with metal ones. This decision was influenced by Parks Department policy, established in 1989, that banned the use of wood in playgrounds because of concerns about durability and maintenance. At community meetings about the project during the summer of 1996, discussions about these changes became contentious. Some community members began to advocate for preserving the playground, forming Friends of the Adventure Playground, which consisted of parents, members from the Upper West Side preservation advocacy group Landmarks West!, and some who had been involved in creating the playground (now grandparents to children who played there). The group was particularly concerned about the plan to replace the wood pyramid with a metal structure, which they believed compromised the integrity of the overall playground design. Parents with a contemporary perspective agreed that wood was preferable but maintained that the advocates' views repudiated the realities of use. To one parent, preserving the playground would be like "GM trying to manufacture a car now that doesn't have seatbelts."[26] Through this debate, the conservancy became more aware of the playground's history, but it did not consult with Richard Dattner until the advocates suggested a meeting. The conservancy presented him with its plans, and in a follow-up letter, Dattner called the project "needed and welcomed" and made suggestions to improve the design.[27] However, in subsequent meetings the debate continued and gained notoriety in the press, which characterized it as a battle between adventure and safety, nostalgia and practicality, and the former and current users.[28]

The ultimate source of this conflict was that the playground, by definition and function, was subject to change. The concerns of the parents from the 1990s were not unlike those of the mothers of the 1960s whose advocacy had resulted in the creation of Adventure Playground: both were responding to the playgrounds of the past and both wanted something new for their children that reflected current ideas about play. The expectation that playgrounds were regularly updated was ingrained in ideas about the park's preservation and even integrated into regulatory policy. During the 1960s, amid the fights against encroachments and growing interest in the park's design and history, administrators had identified playgrounds as the one part of the park that could be modernized. When the city designated the park a Scenic Landmark in 1973, the playgrounds were not included as contributing features. The Landmarks Preservation

FIG. 108
Rebuilding the Adventure Playground pyramid, 1996. The new pyramid was rebuilt to be lower and less steep than the original.

Commission reviewed updates to playgrounds based on their impact on the park, assessing changes to their footprint, fencing, and the surrounding planting and paths—but not the design of the playgrounds themselves.

Friends of the Adventure Playground continued to pressure the conservancy to revise their plans, collecting letters in support of preservation from neighborhood residents, staff from the National Park Service, and a state senator. When the local community board did not approve the plans, asking the conservancy instead to pursue a redesign of the pyramid in wood due to concerns about "design, safety, and appropriateness," the conservancy approached the Parks Department, which agreed to waive the ban on wood on the premise that the conservancy would maintain it.[29] Dattner agreed to work with the conservancy on a design for a new wood pyramid. The final project involved rebuilding the pyramid, tree house, and climbing structure in wood; replacing asphalt and gravel paving with rubber safety surface; adding railings to the main conical climbing feature; and containing the sand to a smaller area. [FIG. 108] Although the scope of work was significant, the most dramatic changes were reduction of the scale and complexity of the wood features. [FIG. 109] The persistence of community members had convinced the conservancy to reconsider Adventure Playground as more than just an old playground in need of an update but as a unique design that embodied innovative ideas about play that were still relevant and to make changes that respected its integrity.

Those advocating to preserve Adventure Playground looked to another controversial project as a model—Public School 166 Playground, located at West 89th Street, which Friedberg had designed in 1968. In

FIG. 109
Adventure Playground, renovated 1997. Following the first renovation, the overall appearance and play experience remained intact.

the mid-1990s, the school proposed demolishing the playground (renamed Playground 89), which had become so deteriorated that it was no longer functional. Neighborhood residents and civic organizations protested these plans, and their pressure led the Parks Department to engage Friedberg to redesign it. Although Friedberg was pleased to be involved, he lamented the circumstances, stating, "We are sanitizing the environment for children under the guise of safety."[30] The new design was less adventurous than his earlier one but still offered similar experiences through a circular amphitheater that incorporated water sprays, a sand play area, and a custom-designed metal climbing structure.

The projects at Adventure Playground and the PS 166 Playground were driven by functional concerns—the need to update them for continued use. Still, some landscape architects and historic preservation professionals viewed the lack of interest in their design integrity and historic significance as part of a larger disregard for modern landscape architecture of the postwar period. This issue was raised at a conference organized by the National Park Service Historic Landscape Initiative (HLI) in 1995 entitled "Preserving Modern Landscape Architecture," which examined the obstacles facing these landscapes and proposed strategies for their renewal and stewardship. Papers provided new scholarship on the work of preeminent midcentury landscape architects, including Dan Kiley, Lawrence Halprin, and James Rose. Three papers addressed playgrounds, including one about the controversial Adventure Playground project in Central Park.[31] This first discussion of playgrounds and historic preservation in an academic context provided a broader context and theoretical framework through which to consider how to update the adventure-style playgrounds and potentially other historic playgrounds.[32]

In his introduction, Charles Birnbaum, the coordinator for HLI and conference curator, examined how insensitive alterations and neglect had compromised the integrity of many postwar landscapes.[33] The Secretary of the Interior's standards for the preservation of buildings and landscapes, developed by the National Park Service, defines integrity as "the authenticity of a property's historic identity, evidenced by the survival of physical characteristics that existed during the property's historic or prehistoric period."[34] Applying this standard to works of landscape architecture can be confounding—much of a landscape's physical components are living and thus dynamic. In a paper on playgrounds, designer Lisa Crowder grappled with the particular challenges of applying the definition of integrity to this typology, which had been demonstrated by the projects at Adventure Playground and PS 166 Playground: "Given the vast changes that have occurred during the past century in our understanding of play and its place in child development and early child education, are 'historically significant' playgrounds so hopelessly outdated and unsafe that their preservation poses a real threat to the intended users? . . . Can their preservation be justified based solely on their place in the design tradition?"[35] Updating historic playgrounds for contemporary use necessitated change to or removal of physical characteristics that inevitably compromised their design integrity. This discussion raised the question of whether the definition of integrity could be broadened to include experience, which was also part of a playground's historic identity. The project at Adventure Playground had involved significant alterations. Yet the updated playground still supported an exploratory and multifaceted play experience that was its original design intent.

Another theme emerging from this conference was how the lack of maintenance had affected the perception and experience of modern landscape architecture. Writing about the plaza designed by landscape architect Dan Kiley at Lincoln Center, which suffered from poor maintenance of plantings, landscape architect Ken Smith attributed this situation to ingrained cultural attitudes and policies about the built environment: "Public works, in particular, are vulnerable because of the common public-policy mentality that favors one-time capital expenditures over ongoing operational and maintenance funding."[36] The deteriorated state of the playgrounds exacerbated concerns about their safety, making it difficult for parents and park administrators to ascertain their value, and thus easier to see demolition as the only option. In a paper about Friedberg's playground designs, landscape designer Alison Dalton emphasized maintenance as "something that must, whenever possible, be negotiated in the design process."[37] Friedberg's PS 166 Playground was a salient illustration of this issue and its origins. Just a few weeks after the playground opened in 1968 with a ceremony attended by Mayor Lindsay, the school's parents' association—which had been instrumental in creating the playground—wrote to the mayor concerned that the "tremendous gift to the city of $225,000 of Astor Foundation funds is in jeopardy of being completely wasted."[38] According to parents, the Parks Department was not maintaining the playground as promised, which was creating safety hazards. Problems with maintenance continued over the years, resulting in the deterioration of play features, and the parents wrote to the Parks Department repeatedly. Out of desperation, in 1975 they contacted the Astor Foundation. The foundation was sympathetic but declined to assist, citing this as a widespread problem in the playgrounds they had funded.[39] In 1966, at the outset of the playground revolution, Dattner had acknowledged that custom-built playgrounds necessitated more intensive maintenance but declared, "playgrounds can't be built anymore for maintenance men."[40] Yet lack of maintenance had compromised the playground revolution, and this needed to be a factor in developing an historic preservation approach to those that remained.

Updating the Adventure-Style Playgrounds

The conservancy continued to confront the tension between preservation and change as well as the demands of specialized maintenance in the process of working in the park's remaining adventure-style playgrounds. In 1999, following another conflict with advocacy groups and community members over a project to update the East 72nd Street Playground, the conservancy adopted the strategy first implemented at Adventure Playground for all adventure-style playgrounds: to update them based on careful consideration of their original design and intent. For many of the ensuing projects, which were implemented between 2000 and 2016, this involved dramatic change, and even the demolition of the existing playground and construction of an entirely new playground that incorporated new versions of its character-defining features—mounds, pyramids, and water features—within a layout similar to the original. Other projects involved rebuilding individual features while repairing or retrofitting others. The comprehensive overhaul of these spaces has also allowed for opportunities to build on and enhance their designs, introduce new features, and to make major upgrades to infrastructure, largely untouched since the playgrounds were built in the 1930s.

Projects such as these are difficult to categorize according to the Secretary of Interior's standards for preservation treatment of historic landscapes. Those that involve minimal change to the playground's distinctive features and layout are generally referred to as rehabilitations, defined as "the act or process of making possible a compatible use for a property through repair, alterations, and additions while preserving those portions or features which convey its historical, cultural, or architectural values."[41] However, rehabilitation does not convey the scope of those projects that have involved the removal of almost all the original playground and the building of an entirely new playground from the ground up. For such projects, the conservancy has used the term reconstruction to convey the extent of the work, reflecting the general sense of the word—not the preservation treatment, which denotes the re-creation of features or structures that have not survived and for the purposes of representing a specific period of time in the landscape's history. The preservation standards for historic landscapes emphasize retaining as much original fabric as possible; in its work on the adventure-style playgrounds, the conservancy's focus has been to retain a continuity of experience.

Notable efforts outside of Central Park to update historic playgrounds reveal a similarly multifaceted and interpretative approach. One comparable example is the rehabilitation of Mitchell Park in Palo Alto,

FIG. 110
"Gopher holes" in Mitchell Park, designed by Robert Royston. The biomorphic abstraction of artists such as Alexander Calder and Jean Arp inspired the design of several features.

FIG. 111
"Gopher holes" in Mitchell Park following rehabilitation, 2008.

California, which was completed in 2002. Landscape architect Robert Royston designed the park, which was completed in 1957 and which is one of several park projects he designed in the Bay Area between 1945 and 1965.[42] Royston's interest in sculpture, abstract painting, and theater design informed his approach to park design, which in Mitchell Park was seen in the numerous unique play features, including a play apartment house, bear sculptures, and the more abstract "gopher holes." [FIG. 110] In the late 1990s, the city's Parks Department proposed a necessary overhaul, which aimed to update the deteriorated playground with new equipment and to comply with design standards.[43] This plan was well received by park users, but when one community member began to advocate an approach that focused on preserving its historic design and features, the broader community, and ultimately the city, became convinced this was an important direction to explore. The Parks Department hired Dillingham Associates Landscape Architects as a consultant and together they considered a variety of options, including preserving the play features as if they were works of art in a museum and making them off-limits to the public. After deciding to prioritize use, they adopted a rehabilitation approach and collaborated with Royston on a plan to repair some features, remove others, and add new ones. Even though the project resulted in significant alterations to the historic fabric,

FIG. 112
Isamu Noguchi, *Playscape* in Piedmont Park, 2017. Noguchi conceived of the playground as a collection of individual sculptural features whose forms and colors corresponded with one another.

the playground still captured Royston's intent to create a cohesively designed child's world, full of captivating and unexpected play features. [FIG. 111]

The preservation of Isamu Noguchi's *Playscape,* the only playground realized in the artist's lifetime, is another relevant example. [FIG. 112] Noguchi designed the playground in 1976 for Atlanta's Piedmont Park, the city's largest park, notable for its early twentieth-century design by the Olmsted Brothers (Frederick Law Olmsted's sons). *Playscape* consisted primarily of freestanding equipment—Noguchi's reinterpretation of swings, slides, and monkey bars. Over time, the equipment deteriorated, creating safety hazards, and the city made several alterations and repairs. In 2007, the city's Department of Parks, Recreation, and Cultural Affairs began planning a more comprehensive project and worked with the Piedmont Park Conservancy, the Noguchi Foundation, and parent groups to achieve consensus on an approach. The city ultimately decided to prioritize the playground as a work of art. The city's Public Art Program, working with consulting art conservators, oversaw the project, which consisted of reversing past alterations, repairing some features, and modifying others to comply with safety standards. When some changes for compliance were deemed too destructive, the city decided to "grandfather" those features.[44]

These examples illustrate how updating historic playgrounds can be a long and complex process, involving multiple stakeholders, input from the original designer (when possible), and specialized consultants. In Central Park, the conservancy's in-house design office begins these projects with a detailed study of the playground, including research into its history and consultation with the original designer, surveys of playground users (both adults and children), an analysis of compliance with safety and accessibility standards, and a detailed conditions assessment. Out of this planning phase, landscape architects develop a preliminary design, which is then presented to the original designer(s) for feedback. As part of the public review process for all design projects in Central Park, the proposed work is presented to all the community boards surrounding the park, civic groups, the Landmarks Preservation Commission, and the Public Design Commission. Their comments are incorporated into the final design. (If their feedback involves extensive changes, the project will require another round of review.) In addition to planning and design, the conservancy also oversees the construction process, including hiring and managing the contractors—a close relationship that is important for building complex, site-constructed play features. The projects typically take two to three years to complete and range in cost from $1 million to $3 million. As in the past, private funding has been critical in undertaking the work, which, relative to traditional playgrounds, is costly. The motivations of donors to fund these renewal projects has remained consistent with those who supported playgrounds in the 1960s and 1970s—an investment in children, community, and the park. Recognizing that playgrounds necessitate ongoing and specialized stewardship, in 1990 the conservancy formed Playground Partners, a program to support maintenance efforts as well as build community around playgrounds.

The projects to update adventure-style playgrounds have benefited from and contributed to renewed attention to playgrounds both in the park and in the city. In 2011, the conservancy completed a planning document entitled *Plan for Play,* which involved an in-depth study of the history, design, and evolution of play and playgrounds in the park. Grounded in this research, and in the conservancy's work in the park since

1980, the document identified consistent goals and design objectives to guide a program of work to rebuild or renovate all of the park's twenty-one playgrounds over the course of a decade.[45] The conservancy's approach drew from contemporary discourse around playgrounds, which has been informed by the nationwide children's health crisis, concerns about the developmental effects of a lack of exposure to natural environments, and backlash against the focus on playground safety resulting in what some critics have characterized as "overprotected" children.[46] New York's efforts, beginning in the mid-2000s, to build new parks, to increase access to recreational opportunities, and to create destination playgrounds, such as Imagination Playground in downtown Manhattan, were a targeted response to these concerns about urban childhood, and these and other initiatives have made playgrounds more central to discussions about the city's vitality. The resurgence of interest in adventure-style playgrounds since the early 2000s has made them a historic precedent for approaches to innovative and child-centered design, while the conservancy's efforts to update them has contributed to greater awareness of their history and relevance.

Adventure-Style Playgrounds and Central Park

Work on Heckscher Playground, completed in 2006, reflected how the playground's relationship to the surrounding park was another primary consideration in updating adventure-style playgrounds. The project was part of an extensive restoration of the area known as the Historic Playground Landscape owing to the long-standing concentration of amenities for children in this part of the park, which in addition to Heckscher Playground includes baseball fields (located on part of the site of the original playground) and the carousel, added in the early 1870s. [FIG. 113]

Heckscher Playground included the two discrete sections designed by Dattner, the one known in the 1970s as the Water Playground and the other a small area with several linked climbing structures set in sand. The rest of the playground remained unchanged since the 1930s, a vast and undefined expanse of asphalt with traditional equipment scattered throughout. [FIG. 114] The conservancy approached the update to Dattner's designs as a rehabilitation, which involved selective rebuilding of play features, upgrading the water infrastructure, and installing new equipment. Work in the rest of the playground was intended to knit the various sections together. To enliven the large area of asphalt paving in the center of the

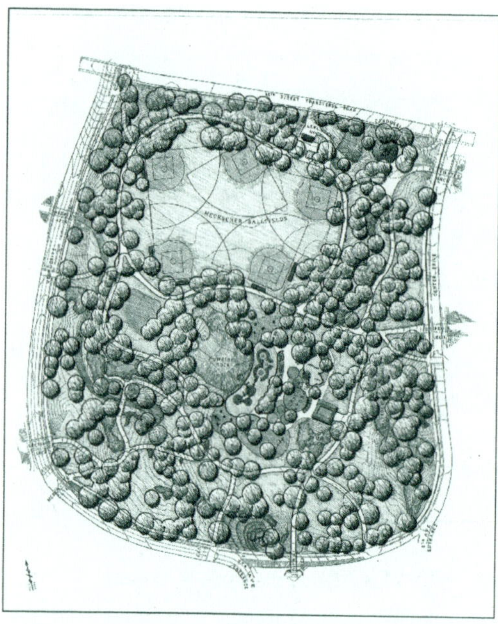

FIG. 113
Plan for the Historic Playground Landscape, 2003. The project to update Heckscher Playground sought to connect it to the broader landscape and the other amenities and experiences for children in the area.

playground while still accommodating an open space for games, the conservancy installed colored safety surface and synthetic turf in circular forms that evoke those in the water playground. On the south and north sides, the focus was on creating transitional zones to lessen the boundary between playground and park using plantings, wood chips for surfacing, and a low wood fence to mark the perimeter. [FIG. 115] Building on the connection to the park that Dattner had made by linking the Water Playground to the rock outcrop that forms its backdrop, these interventions made the entire playground appear more cohesive and connected to the park. [FIG. 116]

Creating physical and visual connections to the park became a guiding principle in all subsequent playground projects, indicative of how the relationship between playground and park has evolved. Olmsted and Vaux designed the park as a space without perceived boundaries, an utmost alternative to the crowded and densely built city and intended to facilitate an experience of what Olmsted described as "a sense of enlarged freedom."[47] The park's playgrounds, created to contain and safeguard children, were defined by rigid enclosures. The modern designs of the

FIG. 114
Heckscher Playground, 2004. Relics of the Moses era were still present when the conservancy began planning the project to update Heckscher Playground.

FIG. 115
Heckscher Playground, 2010. Conservancy landscape architects carefully considered the design of the playground's edges, attempting to make a seamless transition between playground and park.

FIG. 116
Heckscher Playground, 2010. The project in the park's largest and most important historic playground set a precedent for how to make playgrounds feel more integrated into the park.

adventure-style playgrounds further accentuated this disconnect between playground and park. The artist Robert Smithson noted this remoteness on a walk through the park that he chronicled in his essay "Frederick Law Olmsted and the Dialectical Landscape" (1973). He encountered Ancient Play Garden, "one of the latest incursions into the park," which he described as "a pastiche of Philip Johnson and Mark di Suvero. A sign on the fence that surrounds it exhorted one to 'Enjoy.'"[48] Smithson presciently interpreted the park as an earthwork—a work of art and an ecological system under the constant sway of time and human interaction—within which playgrounds appeared static and contrived. Smithson was writing in 1973 when the park's condition was worsening, and he noted trash, drainage problems, and graffiti. These conditions magnified the playground's status as an island, making it retreat from the park itself. Decades later, in the context of a restored Central Park, the conservancy was attempting to make playgrounds feel and appear like an extension of the park.

Working with Safety Standards

Updating these playgrounds for contemporary uses has involved careful consideration of current standards for safety. During the planning process, some community groups have lamented proposed changes necessitated by safety standards, reflecting a view of standards as excessive and evidence of a litigious society that has resulted in the over-reliance on equipment with limited play value. Christopher Nolan, chief landscape architect for the conservancy, who has been involved in all these projects, regards working with the standards as a professional responsibility that does not preclude good design. The standards are one of many constraints that inform the design process. That the standards are open to interpretation is particularly evident when working in adventure-style playgrounds: they are written for play equipment, so applying them to unique, site-constructed features such as a wood pyramid or a concrete wall requires problem-solving and flexibility.

In 2009, the conservancy completed a project in Ancient Play Garden (now known as Ancient Playground), which necessitated creative solutions to make the playground compliant with safety and accessibility standards. The playground was a dense assortment of wood, brick, and concrete features, making it impossible to retrofit the existing forms to comply with the standard requiring a use zone, a defined open space

FIG. 117
Ancient Playground before reconstruction, 2009. Contemporary safety standards required greater distances between play features than existed in Ancient Playground.

around equipment, intended to reduce conflict between play activities. There was simply not enough room. [FIG. 117] Conservancy landscape architects realized that redesigning many of the play features to be slightly smaller and linked together, creating one large composite feature with a use zone surrounding it, would diminish the space requirements.[49] [FIGS. 118 AND 119]

Some advocates and critics viewed the extensive changes to this playground, specifically to the materiality and form of its signature features, as overly compromising its integrity.[50] In general, those who have written about the history and design of these playgrounds typically characterize the changes to them in terms of loss. Writing about these projects in a catalog of historic innovative playgrounds, urban planner and curator Gabriela Burkhalter asserted "the designs lost much of their original idiosyncrasy when they were adapted to meet contemporary security standards."[51] In an essay about the preservation of playgrounds, author Susan Solomon found the changes to Ancient Playground unsettling and criticized the new climbing mounds, which were slightly lower and flatter than the originals, calling them "a cartoonish version of what Dattner had first designed."[52] Paige Johnson, the writer and editor of *Playscapes,* an influential blog about playground design and history, also lamented the loss of original fabric but offered a more balanced assessment through an analysis of the play she witnessed in the new playground: "There was great play going on here. . . . Everywhere you looked there were kids pulling themselves up, and lowering themselves down, tilted surfaces."[53] Johnson's

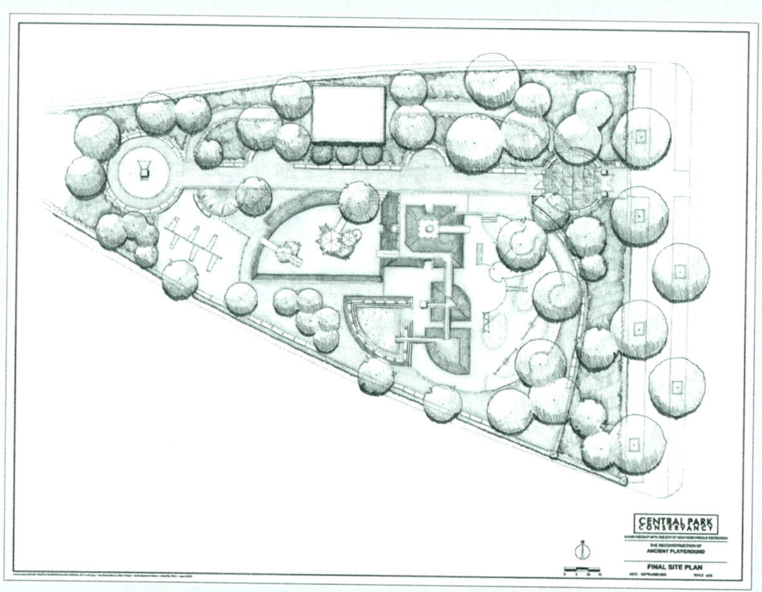

FIG. 118
Site plan for Ancient Playground, 2006. Conservancy landscape architects redesigned the main play features to be linked together.

FIG. 119
Construction in Ancient Playground, 2009. After redesigning the main play features, the only remaining original fabric was the obelisk.

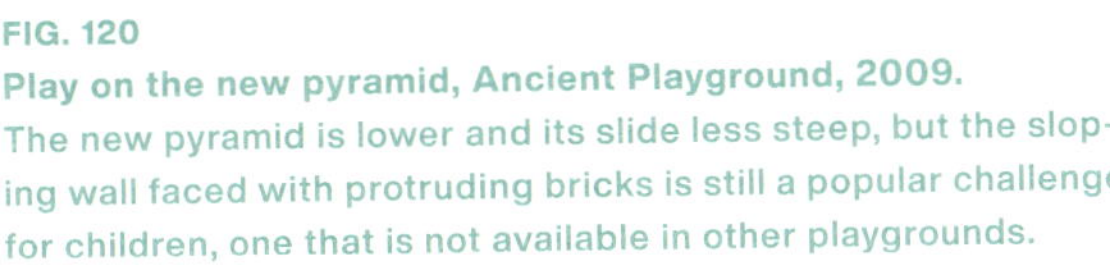

FIG. 120
Play on the new pyramid, Ancient Playground, 2009. The new pyramid is lower and its slide less steep, but the sloping wall faced with protruding bricks is still a popular challenge for children, one that is not available in other playgrounds.

FIG. 121
Water feature, Ancient Playground, 2009. The conservancy focused on preserving the experiences innovated in the adventure-style playgrounds—of linked play, exploring a variety of materials, and of dynamic interactions with water.

observations are a recognition of the aim of this work—sometimes overshadowed by a focus on original fabric and details—to preserve the experience of scampering up a brick-faced pyramid, hiding inside a tunnel, frolicking with cascading water, and jumping from one feature to another. [FIGS. 120 AND 121] These projects are inevitably a compromise; Dattner was also disappointed that Ancient Playground had to change, but he also appreciated its renewal, which made possible its ongoing use.[54]

Preserving Materials: Sand

Advocates for adventure-style playgrounds have also criticized the reduction of sand resulting from these projects. In an article about the initial project in Adventure Playground, Michael Gotkin stated that "the major, and perhaps most damaging, change to the original design integrity was the decision to restrict the broad expanse of sand to a smaller, more contained area, a change that greatly altered the appearance and programmatic intent of the playground design."[55] This assessment was a testament to the value of this material in the original conception of the playground. Although sand had been present in playgrounds since their invention, in the adventure-style playgrounds it was used in unprecedented ways and

FIG. 122
Adventure Playground, 1969.
Sand covered most of the ground in Adventure Playground and other adventure-style playgrounds.

quantities. Designers included sand in large expanses to provide a soft cushioning in case of a fall and to demarcate the play space as a distinct children's world. [FIG. 122] Furthermore, the abundance of sand was emblematic of the purpose of these playgrounds to provide opportunities for creative and manipulative play, a tangible connection to the European adventure playgrounds. Lady Allen of Hurtwood extolled the inclusion of sand (and water) to accommodate children's innate desires to transform their environment, noting that "children of all ages, all over the world, are happiest when they can move things around to their own liking."[56]

Recognizing sand as significant original fabric and experience, the conservancy has incorporated it into the redesigned playgrounds, although it no longer functions as safety surfacing. This decision was not driven primarily by maintenance. (The conservancy has a daily playground maintenance regime and most of the park's playgrounds contain sand.) In the vicinity of features such as slides or swings, sand regularly gets displaced, becoming less effective as safety surfacing. Furthermore, for some of the same reasons sand is valuable as a play material, it presents a barrier to playground users that are less able-bodied. In addition

FIG. 123
"Sand carpet" in the Tarr Family Playground (formerly Discovery Play Park), 2009. The carpet retains the appearance of sand but is flat and even.

to safety standards, the Americans with Disabilities Act (ADA) influences the projects to update adventure-style playgrounds. A civil rights law that prohibits discrimination against people with disabilities, the ADA stipulates that public facilities be made physically accessible according to specific guidelines when they are renovated.[57] The ADA Standards for Accessible Design provides technical standards for public playgrounds, including a requirement for accessible routes throughout the playground to allow the disabled to access play equipment or features. Sand surfacing is impossible to traverse in a wheelchair and is challenging for anyone with mobility issues, and removing this barrier is necessary to provide an integrated experience for both children and caregivers.

In an effort to honor the original appearance of sand-surfaced playgrounds while complying with the ADA, the conservancy experimented with a new accessible "sand carpet" made of polypropylene (a type of plastic) in a tan color. [FIG. 123] The carpet is compatible with sand and in fact, sand is raked into it to keep the carpet fibers raised. As part of a project in Discovery Play Park (now known as the Tarr Family Playground) completed in 2009, the conservancy installed this surface and concentrated sand for play in two areas: in the center of the playground and in a new sandbox for toddlers. [FIGS. 124–126] The conservancy's dual role of both designing and maintaining playgrounds allows it to try out new materials and incorporate more maintenance-intensive features.

FIG. 124
"Sea of sand" in the Tarr Family Playground, 2009. The conservancy installed a pile of sand near and under the bridge (on left), making the sand appear contiguous with the safety carpet.

FIG. 125
Sandbox in Discovery Play Park, 1973. The original sandbox and sand sifter provided the inspiration for a new sandbox.

FIG. 126
Sandbox in Tarr Family Playground, 2017. The new sandbox incorporated the original sand sifter and introduced a new feature, a water spigot to accommodate a popular playground activity—mixing sand with water.

FIG. 127
West 110th Street Playground, originally constructed in 1979.

Preserving Materials: Wood

In each of the projects to update the adventure-style playgrounds, the conservancy has included custom-designed features constructed in wood based on the design of climbers, tire swings, tree houses that were prevalent original features. In 2011, the conservancy began a project to rebuild the East 110th Street Playground, which had been constructed by the Parks Department in 1979 entirely with wood equipment similar to TimberForm. [FIG. 127] Although this equipment had deteriorated after thirty years of use, it was still popular, particularly with older children, because it offered a physically challenging play experience. The conservancy aimed to create a new design inspired by the original wood features, and it engaged Columbia Cascade, the original manufacturers of TimberForm, which still produces similar wood equipment. The company's connection to the history of these spaces and decades-long experience with wood informed the approach to design, which ultimately still derived from Friedberg's concept of linked play and his belief that "the more complex the playground, the greater the choice and the more enriched the learning experience."[58] The conservancy designed a new wood feature around a large tree, consisting of stepping forms, bridges, ladders, poles, and a ramp for wheelchair access. [FIG. 128] The feature became an integral part of a completely

FIG. 128
New wood feature in the West 110th Street Playground, 2013.

FIG. 129
East 110th Street Playground, 2013. As with all projects in playgrounds, conservancy landscape architects aimed to connect the playground to the surrounding landscape.

FIG. 130
The tree houses at Discovery Play Park, 1973. The original design consisted of two multi-level tree houses, connected by a rope bridge. The pulley ride was never realized.

reconfigured space, which also included a new water feature and swings. [FIG. 129]

Wood is an ideal material for Central Park's playgrounds, complementing the materials of the park and thus making connections to the larger landscape. During the planning for work in Discovery Play Park, the conservancy recognized that the tree house built around two pin oaks was one of the most important features in the original playground and offered an experience not available to most urban children, but the wood was rotting and treated with preservatives no longer permitted in a public environment. [FIG. 130] The conservancy designed a new tree house around the existing trees, a challenging endeavor because it necessitated engineering footings that did not disturb the trees' extensive root systems. [FIG. 131] Just a few days after the playground reopened, a dramatic windstorm destroyed hundreds of trees in the northern part of Central Park, including the pin oaks in the playground. [FIG. 132] Although the tree house remained intact, it was without its focal point and inspiration, a sobering reminder of the full range of environmental forces that can impact the park and its playgrounds.

FIG. 131
New tree house, inspired by the original design, 2009.

FIG. 132
Storm damage in the Tarr Family Playground, 2009.

FIG. 133
East 72nd Street Playground, before reconstruction, 2009.
The playground's bold geometries appeared crammed into the oval footprint.

Conclusion: Reprise

The conservancy's most recent projects in adventure-style playgrounds, completed in 2015, involved returning to work for a second time in Adventure Playground and East 72nd Street Playground, which were first updated in 1997 and 2000, respectively. These projects mark both a culmination and a turning point in thinking about play and playground design in Central Park. They have benefited from years of experience working in adventure-style playgrounds, a greater awareness of their history and significance, and a focus on the physical context of playgrounds throughout the park. Both projects, which involved removal of original fabric, were well received by advocacy groups who in the past have often expressed apprehension over change, indicative of how the relationship with stakeholders has also evolved.

The project at East 72nd Street Playground involved a comprehensive reevaluation of the playground's relationship to the surrounding park, a process that ended up accentuating one of the more distinctive aspects of its original design. Dattner had designed a low concrete wall with an irregular angular form to demarcate the play space. While this was

FIG. 134
Conceptual plan for the East 72nd Street Playground, 2014. The conservancy redesigned the playground so that the main angular form became the footprint.

FIG. 135
East 72nd Street Playground after completion, 2015. The new footprint accentuated Dattner's forms and allowed more space for plantings surrounding the playground.

FIG. 136
East 72nd Street Playground, 2016. Instead of contrasting with the fence and footprint, the playground's signature forms are in dialogue with the park.

striking, it created an awkward relationship with the playground's oval-shaped footprint. [FIG. 133] Conservancy landscape architects removed the fence that demarcated the perimeter and used Dattner's angular shape to articulate the playground's boundary, which was secured with a low, transparent fence and bordered by numerous new plantings. [FIGS. 134 AND 135] The colors and forms of granite block, concrete, and metal announce the design as emphatically modern; yet the playground has a newfound sense of spaciousness and openness to the park. [FIG. 136]

The recent project at Adventure Playground also embodied an evolution of thinking about these spaces, completed almost forty years after it was built and twenty years after the first project to update it. The work involved a detailed focus on the existing design that balanced a combination of approaches: retrofitting some of the original play features, rebuilding others, and reconstructing some that had been lost. [FIGS. 137–139] A recognition that Adventure Playground is the premier remaining example of the playgrounds from this era informed the focus on preserving as much of the existing design as possible. The fact that it was less densely built than other adventure-style playgrounds made it possible to update it for compliance with safety standards using less-intrusive methods. Comparing photographs of Adventure Playground soon after it opened and photographs of it after the project was completed, it is remarkable how similar they look, and how much the play experience has remained unchanged. [FIG. 140]

One of the most innovative concepts emerging from the playground revolution is that the design of playgrounds should endeavor to reflect children's behavior and experience. Both Dattner and Friedberg emphasized that the study of how children played in the world—in the streets, in empty lots, in natural settings—was their starting point for design. In his book *Play and Interplay*, Friedberg reflected on the child's innate inventiveness and the ideal conditions to encourage this: "He may climb a tree or throw a rope over a branch for a swing or jump from a rock or find water, sand, or tree branches to play with. Or build things. Or demolish things. When the world is open to him, his imagination puts it to good use."[59] The book includes photographs that illustrate how Friedberg "translated" the experience of playing in the world to the design of forms and features for the playground.

Both Friedberg and Dattner endeavored to create play spaces that were open to the imagination—that presented opportunities for choice,

FIG. 137
Illustration of changes to conical climber, Adventure Playground, 2014. The project included restoring access to the tunnels leading into the conical climber, which had been closed in the 1970s because of safety concerns.

FIG. 138
Pouring concrete for the new water feature, Adventure Playground, 2015. The most extensive change was the construction of a new accessible water feature based on the design of the original.

FIG. 139
Adventure Playground, 1967 and in 2017.

FIG. 140
Sliding in an adventure-style playground, 1967.

discovery, and creativity. While they recognized the value of playgrounds as children's worlds, as protected spaces where children could play and explore more safely and immersively than they could in the rest of the urban environment, they also articulated, and Friedberg most emphatically, that playgrounds should relate to and feel connected to urban life. The adventure-style playgrounds achieved this in part through their connections to pioneering ideas about art and design and ideals of urban community. For a brief period, the playgrounds demonstrated the centrality of play to urban culture and animated a city on the brink of disaster.

The history of playgrounds in Central Park demonstrates the tension between playgrounds as inward-focused children's worlds and children as participants in the broader urban landscape, which was manifested spatially through the design of playgrounds and their relationship to the park. The conservancy's work to enhance the physical and visual connections between the playgrounds and the park is a way to open the

FIG. 141
The author's friend Daphne and niece Zola sliding down a rock outcrop in Central Park, 2016.

imagination to what play in the park can be, to inspire children and their caregivers to see that play does not need to be limited to the domain of the playground. In a sense it aims to reverse Friedberg's construct of translation back from playground to park—where there are rocks to climb, sticks to collect, lawns to run across, and no safety standards. [FIG. 141] From the perspective of my eight-year-old friend, Daphne: "A meadow is like a playground. You can do anything here. If you want to swing, you could put it here [pointing to a tree limb]. Meadows are open and peaceful, and you can be free and run around.[60] The beauty of the restored park is the way it announces its essential and timeless purpose as a place for play.

Acknowledgments

The origins of this project and my interest in the history of playgrounds can be traced, not surprisingly, to childhood and my experiences playing in various playgrounds in the East Village, where I grew up, and in other parts of New York City. Decades later, in a graduate course called the Material Culture of Childhood, I remembered these spaces and began to wonder more about origins and design of the concrete turtles and whales in the housing development across the street from our apartment, the dilapidated swings and slides in Tompkins Square Park, and the alluring pyramids and tunnels in the playground in Central Park near the Metropolitan Museum of Art (Ancient Playground, designed by Richard Dattner). With the help of professors Amy Ogata and Timothy Davis, I began to delve into the little-known history of urban spaces for children, as well as the history of public parks in New York City.

After graduate school, I was lucky to land at the Central Park Conservancy, where I became somewhat immersed in playgrounds. Since 2011, the conservancy has been working to update all of Central Park's playgrounds, and through my work on this effort I became interested in the adventure-style playgrounds. My colleagues at the conservancy, Lane Addonizio, Sara Cedar Miller, and Chris Nolan, all cultivated this interest and my idea to further explore it in a book. I deeply appreciate their support of this project and all that they have shared with me about history of Central Park and its ongoing relevance. Charles Birnbaum of the Cultural Landscape Foundation recognized the potential for this topic as a contribution to both the history of Central Park and modern landscape architecture and provided invaluable insights and editorial assistance throughout the process. Marta Gutman generously shared ideas and resources during various phases of this project, and I am also grateful for her encouragement of my work as a historian in other ways.

I have learned a lot about designing, building, and preserving playgrounds from the landscape architects who have worked to update the adventure-style playgrounds, including Gary Dearborn, Liz Kushner, Chris Nolan, Bob Rumsey, Stephanie Saulmon, and David Turner. I am grateful to all those who spent time to share their personal involvement in this history, particularly Richard Dattner and M. Paul Friedberg, whose stories, details, and images made the book so much richer. Many thanks to Lane Addonizio, Sara Cedar Miller, and Charles Birnbaum for reading various drafts, Cara Jordan for editing, and Jenny Burton and Camille Lannan for helping organize images. I thank Kate Papacosma for her help with research and was often inspired by our discussions and shared enthusiasm for playgrounds. Hillary Angelo provided critical comments on a final draft, and I enjoyed our conversations about parks and other public spaces. Rebekah Burgess, photo archivist at the New York City Parks Photo Archive, and her predecessor, Christina Benson, both worked avidly to find numerous historic photographs, which are so critical to telling the story. I greatly appreciate Margaret Lovecraft and Jo Ann Kiser from Louisiana State University Press, as well as the anonymous readers, for all their work to improve and polish the text. A grant from the New York State Council on the Arts supported the research and writing. The Central Park Conservancy also provided support for the publication of this book.

Lastly, I want to acknowledge my friends and family, who were proud and supportive of this effort but at times tired of its demands on my time. I am particularly grateful to my niece Zola Warsh and friend Daphne Sacks for sharing their love of play and perspectives on playgrounds.

Notes

Introduction

1. Charles Mee, "Putting the Play in Playgrounds," *New York Times,* November 6, 1966.
2. Peter Walker and Melanie Simo, *Invisible Gardens: The Search for Modernism in the American Landscape* (Cambridge, MA: MIT Press, 1996), 2–11.
3. Sara Cedar Miller, *Central Park: An American Masterpiece* (New York: Abrams, 2003); David Schuyler, *The New Urban Landscape* (Baltimore: Johns Hopkins University Press, 1993).
4. Park Association, "Citizens View Their Parks," December 1962. Parks Council Records, Avery Architectural and Fine Arts Library, Columbia University.
5. *Parks and Recreation,* campaign white paper issued by John Lindsay (New York, 1965).
6. Richard Dattner, *Design for Play* (New York: Van Nostrand/Reinhold, 1969); M. Paul Friedberg with Ellen Perry Berkeley, *Play and Interplay: A Manifesto for New Design in Urban Recreational Environment* (New York: Macmillan, 1970).
7. Bruce Kovner, "101 Signs That the City Isn't Dying," *New York Magazine,* February 7, 1972, 31–40.
8. Susan Solomon includes histories of various innovative play spaces created during the 1960s and 1970s as part of a broader discussion about contemporary playground design and strategies for improving it in *American Playgrounds: Revitalizing Community Space* (Hanover, NH: University Press of New England, 2005). A 2012 exhibition about design for children at the Museum of Modern Art included examples of these and other innovative playgrounds; Tanya Harrod, Medea Hoch, and Juliet Kinchin, *Century of the Child: Growing by Design 1900–2000* (New York: Museum of Modern Art, 2012). The Playground Project, an exhibition mounted in 2013 as part of the Carnegie International in Pittsburgh, presented an international scope for the playground revolution; Gabriela Burkhalter, *The Playground Project* (Zurich: JRP|Ringier, 2016). The influential blog about innovative playground design, www.play-scapes.com, includes many posts about adventure-style playgrounds. James Trainor chronicles the adventure-style playgrounds of New York in "Reimagining Recreation," *Cabinet* 45 (Spring 2012); *http://cabinetmagazine.org/issues/45/trainor.php* (accessed June 24, 2017).
9. Central Park Conservancy, *Plan for Play* (New York: Central Park Conservancy, 2011).

Chapter 1

1. "Creative Playground Begun in Central Park," *New York Times,* October 12, 1966.
2. Philippe Aries, *Centuries of Childhood: A Social History of Family Life,* trans. Robert Baldick (New York: Vintage, 1962); Marta Gutman and Ning de Coninck-Smith, eds., *Designing Modern Childhoods: History, Space, and the Material Culture of Children* (New Brunswick, NJ: Rutgers University Press, 2008); Tanya Harrod, Medea Hoch, and Juliet Kinchin, *Century of the Child: Growing by Design 1900–2000* (New York: Museum of Modern Art, 2012).
3. Committee for a Creative Playground, Newsletter 1, no. 1 (April 1966). Lauder Archives.
4. Steven A. Riess, *City Games: The Evolution of American Urban Society and the Rise of Sports* (Urbana: University of Illinois Press, 1989), 13.
5. Board of Commissioners of the Central Park, *Fifth Annual Report* (New York: William C. Bryant & Co., 1861), 42–49.
6. Board of Commissioners of the Central Park, *Third Annual Report* (New York: William C. Bryant & Co., 1859), 36.

7. Frederick Law Olmsted and Calvert Vaux, "A Review of Recent Changes, and Changes Which Have Been Projected, in the Plans of the Central Park" (1872), in *Forty Years of Landscape Architecture,* ed. Frederick Law Olmsted Jr. and Theodora Kimball (Cambridge, MA: MIT Press, 1973), 248.
8. Board of Commissioners of the Central Park, *Sixth Annual Report* (New York: William C. Bryant & Co., 1863), 55–56.
9. Board of Commissioners of the Central Park, *Tenth Annual Report* (New York: William C. Bryant & Co., 1868), 37; Board of Commissioners of the Central Park, *Eleventh Annual Report* (New York: William C. Bryant & Co., 1868), 26–27, 114.
10. Charles F. Wingate, "Amusements at the Central Park," *Appleton's Journal* 8 (August 3, 1873): 129.
11. Board of Commissioners of the Central Park, *Tenth Annual Report* (New York: William C. Bryant & Co, 1867), 38.
12. Ibid.
13. On the playground movement, see Paul Boyer, *Urban Masses and Moral Order in America, 1820–1920* (Cambridge, MA: Harvard University Press, 1978); Dominick Cavallo, *Muscles and Morals: Organized Playgrounds and Urban Reform, 1880–1920* (Philadelphia: University of Pennsylvania Press, 1981).
14. Joe L. Frost, *Play and Playscapes* (Albany, NY: Delmar Publishers, 1992), 113–14.
15. Roger Hart, "Containing Children: Some Lessons on Planning for Play from New York City," in *Environment and Urbanization* 14, no 2 (October 2002): 135–48.
16. For the small parks movement, see Marie Warsh, "Cultivating Citizens: The Children's School Farm in New York City: 1902–1931," *Buildings and Landscapes* 18, no. 1 (Spring 2011): 64–89.
17. The first municipally funded playground in the United States was Charlesbank Playground in Boston, which opened in 1899. The playground was part of the series of parks known as the Emerald Necklace designed by Olmsted with Charles Eliot, John Charles Olmsted, and Frederick Law Olmsted Jr. between 1878 and 1895. See Cynthia Zaitzesky, *Frederick Law Olmsted and the Boston Park System* (Cambridge, MA: Belknap Press, 1992), 96–101.
18. Warsh, "Cultivating Citizens."
19. Joseph Lee, *Constructive and Preventive Philanthropy* (New York: Macmillan, 1902), 123.
20. Events in parks were chronicled in the Parks Department's annual reports. See Department of Parks: Boroughs of Manhattan and Richmond, *Report on Public Park Playgrounds and Recreation Centres* (New York: Office of Bureau of Recreation, 1912).
21. "Plans Drawn for Great Park Changes," *New York Times,* July 1, 1910.
22. "Fifty Years Fight to Keep Central Park from Invasion," *New York Times,* July 10, 1910; "Urge City against Popularizing Parks," *New York Times,* March 23, 1911.
23. "Can't Change the Park without Parsons," *New York Times,* July 3, 1910.
24. "If 'Improvement' Plans Had Gobbled Central Park," *New York Times Magazine,* March 31, 1918; Olmsted Jr. and Kimball, *Forty Years,* 519–32.
25. R. L. Duffus, "Central Park Playgrounds Stir Old Issue," *New York Times,* May 10, 1925; "Construction of Central Park Playground under Heckscher Gift Progresses," *New York Times,* November 8, 1925.
26. Hermann W. Merkel, *Report on Survey of Central Park with Recommendations* (New York: Department of Parks, 1927), 7, 17.
27. Hilary Ballon and Kenneth T. Jackson, eds., *Robert Moses and the Modern City: The Transformation of New York* (New York: W. W. Norton & Co., 2007).
28. These events were announced in Parks Department press releases, 1934–60, available on the Parks Departments website: https://www.nycgovparks.org/news/reports/archive#pr (accessed June 24, 2017).
29. Department of Parks, *5 Years of Progress* (New York: Department of Parks, 1939), 29.
30. Margaret Russell, "A New Playground in a City Park," *New York Times,* April 11, 1937.
31. Department of Parks, *26 Years of Progress* (New York: Department of Parks, 1960), n.p.
32. Department of Parks, *18 Years of Progress* (New York: Department of Parks, 1952), 29.
33. Marta Gutman, "Equipping the Public Realm:

Rethinking Robert Moses and Recreation," in *Robert Moses and the Modern City,* 72–85.

34. "Perimeter Playgrounds," *New York Times,* September 14, 1935.
35. Olmsted Jr. and Kimball, *Forty Years,* 156–68.
36. Lewis Mumford, "The Sky Line: Parks and Playgrounds—New Buildings for Old," October 24, 1936, in *Sidewalk Critic: Lewis Mumford's Writings on New York* (New York: Princeton Architectural Press, 1998), 168.
37. "Padlocks Ordered for Playgrounds," *New York Times,* February 16, 1937.
38. The Battle of Central Park is covered in Robert Caro, *The Power Broker: Robert Moses and the Fall of New York* (New York: Knopf, 1974), 984–1004; and John B. Keely, *Moses on the Green* (University: University of Alabama Press, 1959).
39. "37 Fight for a Bit of Central Park," *New York Times,* April 14, 1956.
40. "Central Park Mothers Vanquish Bulldozer Set to Raze Play Area," *New York Times,* April 18, 1956.
41. Elizabeth Blackmar and Roy Rosenzweig, *The Park and the People* (New York: Henry Holt, 1992), 482; Richard Dattner, *Design for Play* (New York: Van Nostrand/Reinhold, 1969), 65; James Trainor, "Reimagining Recreation" *Cabinet* 45 (Spring 2012), *http://cabinetmagazine.org/issues/45/trainor.php* (accessed June 24, 2017).
42. "Group's Demand for a Playground Attendant Is Cut Short by Police," *New York Times,* October 6, 1956; "Mothers Renew Fight for Park Guards, Sending Protests to Wagner and Moses," *New York Times,* October 8, 1956.
43. Department of Parks, *12 Years of Progress* (New York: Department of Parks, 1945), 6–7; Department of Parks, *28 Years of Progress* (New York: Department of Parks, 1962), 41–42.
44. Department of Parks, *28 Years of Progress,* 42.
45. Dattner, *Design for Play,* 65; Committee for a Creative Playground, Newsletter, April 1966, Adventure Playground files, Lauder Archive.
46. "Central Park Playground Testing a Safety Cushion, *New York Times,* July 25, 1963; Department of Parks, *30 Years of Progress* (New York: Department of Parks, 1964), 5.
47. Mothers Committee to Improve the West 67th Street Playground, "An Agenda for the Improvement of the West 67th Street Playground," undated, Central Park files, 1966, Administration Files of the Department of Parks, Municipal Archives (hereafter Municipal Archives).
48. Committee for a Creative Playground, Newsletter, April 1966. Adventure Playground files, Lauder Archive.

Chapter 2

1. "Central Park Playground Puts Fun over Asphalt," *New York Times,* May 26, 1967.
2. Park Association of New York City, *The Playground Revolution* (New York: Park Association, 1966).
3. Ibid., n.p.
4. *Parks and Recreation,* campaign white paper issued by John Lindsay (New York, 1965).
5. For Dattner's biography and career, see Richard Dattner and Partner Architects, *Richard Dattner: Selected and Current Works of Richard Dattner and Partners Architects* (Mulgrave, Victoria: Images, 2001).
6. "Beauty and Fashion Leader, Estée Lauder Founds the Estée and Joseph Lauder Foundation," Press Release, December 1962. Adventure Playground files, Lauder Archives.
7. Douglas E. Kneeland, "City Accepts 'Adventure Playground' in Central Park," *New York Times,* June 9, 1966.
8. Charles Mee, "Putting the Play in Playgrounds," *New York Times,* November 6, 1966; Arthur Rosenblatt, "Recreation: A Chance for Innovative Design," *Architectural Record* (August 1967): 120; Jay Jacobs, "Projects for Playgrounds," *Art in America* (November/December 1967): 51; Alfred Ledermann and Alfred Trachsel, *Creative Playgrounds and Recreation Centers* (New York: Frederick A. Praeger, 1968), 96–99.
9. Richard Dattner, *Design for Play* (New York: Van Nostrand/Reinhold, 1969), 44.
10. Jane Jacobs, *The Death and Life of Great American Cities* (New York: Vintage Books, 1961), 13.
11. Ibid., 50.
12. Ibid., 81.
13. William H. Whyte (1971–1999) was an author and urbanist known for his observation and

study of social behavior in various urban settings, which he documented in *The Social Life of Small Urban Spaces* (Washington, DC: Conservation Foundation, 1980).

Urban planner Kevin Lynch (1918–1984) influenced understanding of the perceptual experience of urban environments in books such as *Image of the City* (Cambridge, MA: MIT Press, 1960). For the relationship between urban design and theory, see Mariana Mogilevich, "Designing the Urban: Space and Politics in Lindsay's New York" (PhD diss., Harvard University, 2012).

14. Quoted in Roy Kozlovsky, "Adventure Playgrounds and Postwar Construction," in Marta Gutman and Ning de Coninck-Smith, eds., *Designing Modern Childhoods* (New Brunswick, NJ: Rutgers University Press, 2008); 174.
15. Kozlovsky, "Adventure Playgrounds,"171–90.
16. Lady Allen of Hurtwood, *Planning for Play* (London: Thames & Hudson, 1968), 55.
17. Kozlovsky, "Adventure Playgrounds,"184.
18. Ibid., 174.
19. For additional examples of adventure playgrounds, see Arvid Bengtsson, *Adventure Playgrounds* (London: Crosby Lockwood Staples, 1973); Clare C. Cooper, "Adventure Playgrounds," *Landscape Architecture* 61 (October 1970): 18–29, 88–91.
20. *Parks and Recreation,* 3.
21. Marie Warsh, "An Introduction to the Adventure Playgrounds of New York," *Plot: Waste Stream* 4 (Spring 2015): 26–34.
22. David M. Grant, "With a Hop, Skip and Jump, Playgrounds Go Modern," *New York Times,* June 17, 1973.
23. Ibid.
24. Dattner, *Design for Play,* 65.
25. Richard Dattner, "Design Objectives for Adventure Playground," June 8, 1956. Adventure Playground files, Lauder archives.
26. Emma Harrison, "Shouts of Children Echo Again in Revived Uptown Playground," *New York Times,* August 8, 1960.
27. Isamu Noguchi, *Isamu Noguchi: Essays and Conservations* (New York: Abrams, 1994), 137.
28. Shaina D. Larrivee, "Playscapes: Isamu Noguchi's Design for Play," *Public Art Dialogue* 1 (2001): 53–80.
29. Tom Hess, "The Rejected Playground," *Art News* 51 (April 1952): 15.
30. Noguchi, *Essays and Conversations,* 126.
31. "Summary of Priorities for Proposed Playground and Recreation Area," undated. Riverside Park Playground files, Noguchi Archives, Isamu Noguchi Foundation and Garden Museum (hereafter Noguchi Archives).
32. Letter from Newbold Morris to Helen Morris, United Neighborhood Houses of New York, February 20, 1962. Noguchi Archives.
33. Barry Benepe, "Riverside Park's Future," *West Side News,* January 27, 1966.
34. In March 1964, *Progressive Architecture* featured the playground on the cover accompanying the article "New Report: Kahn-Noguchi Playground Proposed for New York" (March 1964): 67. It was also included in one of the earliest publications on modern landscape architecture (Elizabeth B. Kassler, *Modern Gardens and the Landscape* [New York: Museum of Modern Art, 1964]).
35. Ralph Blumenthal, "Fight over Park Nearing Climax," *New York Times,* February 13, 1966; Robert E. Tomasson, "City Is Enjoined on a Playground," *New York Times,* April 28, 1966.
36. Tomasson, "City Is Enjoined."
37. See Solomon, *American Playgrounds,* 49; Ana Maria Torres, *Isamu Noguchi: A Study of Space* (New York: Monacelli Press, 2000), 147.
38. A year before the Battle of Central Park, a group of bird watchers successfully fought a proposal to build a senior center in the woodland landscape known as the Ramble. In 1958, West Village residents prevailed over plans to construct a highway through Washington Square. Moses dismissed the protestors as "a bunch of mothers." See Murray Illson, "Bird-Lovers Balk at Moses Project," *New York Times,* October 2, 1955; Robert Fishman, "Revolt of the Urbs: Robert Moses and His Critics," in *Moses and the Modern City,* 122–29; Anthony Wood, *Preserving New York: Winning the Right to Protect a City's Landmarks* (New York: Routledge, 2008), 59.
39. *Parks and Recreation,* 6, 11.
40. Dattner, *Design for Play,* 66.
41. Alison Hirsch, "From 'Open Space' to 'Public Space': Activist Landscape Architects of the

1960s," *Landscape Journal* 33, no. 2 (2014): 174–94.

42. Mee, "Putting the Play in Playgrounds."
43. On Creative Playthings, see Amy Ogata, *Designing the Creative Child: Playthings and Places in Midcentury America* (Minneapolis: University of Minnesota Press, 2013), 57–64.
44. Ibid., 59.
45. Other examples of sculptures for children added during the Moses era include Sophie Loeb Fountain (1936), which also depicted *Alice in Wonderland; Mother Goose* (1938); the gates to the Osborn Playground by Paul Manship with scenes from *Aesop Fables* (1956); *Hans Christian Anderson* (1956); and the various statues of animals at the Zoo, which was expanded in 1935.
46. Jacobs, "Projects for Playgrounds," 50.
47. Joe Frost, *A History of Children's Play and Play Environments* (New York: Routledge, 2010), 180–83.
48. For Friedberg's biography and career, see M. Paul Friedberg, Oral History Interview (Washington, DC: The Cultural Landscape Foundation, 2009); Paul Bennett, "Social Force: The Urban Optimism of M. Paul Friedberg," in *Preserving Modern Landscape Architecture II: Making Postwar Landscape Visible* (Washington, DC: Spacemaker Press, 2004): 32–37.
49. Ira S. Robbins, "Open Space in Public Housing—The New Approach," in *Small Urban Spaces,* ed.Whitney North Seymour Jr. (New York: New York University Press, 1969), 29–39; Nicholas Dagan Bloom, *Public Housing That Worked: New York in the Twentieth Century* (Philadelphia: University of Pennsylvania, 2009), 153–66.
50. Bloom, *Public Housing,* 163.
51. "Making Public Housing Human," *Progressive Architecture* 46, no. 1 (January 1965): 177–79.
52. "Mrs. Astor Sponsors Outdoor Living Rooms," *Washington Post,* March 6, 1966.
53. M. Paul Friedberg, *Playgrounds for City Children* (Washington, DC: Association for Childhood Education International, 1969), 20.
54. M. Paul Friedberg with Ellen Perry Berkeley, *Play and Interplay: A Manifesto for New Design in Urban Recreational Environment* (New York: Macmillan, 1970), 40.
55. Lisa Hammel, "Playing Is More than Just Fun and Games," *New York Times,* August 14, 1967.
56. Friedberg's description of Riis Plaza playground in Museum of Contemporary Crafts, "Objects in the Open Air," Press Release, April 1, 1966, 3. American Craft Council Library and Archives, Digital Collection.
57. John Moss Dixon, "Riis Plaza: Three Acres Filled with Life," *Architectural Forum* (July–August 1966): 68–73; "Urban Playscapist," *Progressive Architecture* (August 1966): 70–72. An article about Thomas Hoving in *Life* magazine featured numerous photos of the commissioner in the playground, which he called his favorite: "Outdoorsman of the Big City," *Life* (April 29, 1966), 39–42.
58. Letter from Mrs. Lyndon B. Johnson to Brooke Astor, May 24, 1966. Box 8, Riis Park, 1965. Vincent Astor Foundation records, Manuscripts and Archives Division, the New York Public Library. (Hereafter VAF records.)
59. Ada Louise Huxtable, "At Last, a Winner," *New York Times,* May 24, 1966.

Chapter 3

1. Central Park files, 1966, Municipal Archives.
2. "Hoving Wants Budget Cuts Restored," May 5, 1966, Department of Parks Press Release.
3. "Outdoorsman of the Big City," *Life* (April 29, 1966): 42; Bernard Weinraub, "A Happening Called Hoving," *New York Times,* July 10, 1966.
4. For a summary of the Parks Department's approach to design in this period, see Arthur Rosenblatt, "Recreation: A Chance for Innovative Urban Design," *Architectural Record* (August 1967): 109–24.
5. "Hoving to Name Curators to Beautify City's Parks," *New York Times,* December 12, 1965. Although Reed's position was ultimately somewhat nominal—he was not paid and was not regularly consulted on park affairs—he was successful in raising awareness about Central Park's history, authoring a guidebook and leading walking tours of the park. See Reed, *Central Park: A History and Guide* (New York: C. N. Potter, 1967).
6. Douglas E. Kneeland, "City Accepts 'Adventure

Playground' in Central Park," *New York Times,* June 9, 1966.

7. August Heckscher, *Alive in the City: Memoir of an Ex-Commissioner* (New York: Scribner, 1974), 258.
8. "Summer Romance," *Newsweek* 68 (July 18, 1966).
9. Don McNeill, "Central Park Rite Is Medieval Pageant," *Village Voice,* March 30, 1967, 1, 20.
10. For the role of the arts in city life and policy during this period, see Mariana Mogilevich, "Arts as Public Policy: Cultural Spaces for Democracy and Growth," in *Summer in the City,* ed. Joseph Viteritti (Baltimore: Johns Hopkins University Press, 2014), 195–222.
11. PRCA *Annual Report 1967* (New York: PRCA, 1968).
12. *Sculpture in Environment* (New York: PRCA, 1967), n.p.
13. "I still think it's a fun city" was a comment Lindsay made in response to the 1966 transit strike. Dick Schaap, "The Fun City," *New York Herald Tribune,* January 7, 1966.
14. McCandlish Phillips, "Couple Quietly Fixes Up Play Yard (Central Park)," *New York Times,* September 28, 1967.
15. Letter from Mel Daus, director of recreation, to Mr. Yutlzler, September 20, 1966; Department of Parks Memo on Improvement to the West 81st Street Playground, September 23, 1966; Letter from Constance Eiseman to Arthur Rosenblatt, November 28, 1966. Central Park Files, 1966, Municipal Archives.
16. Phillips, "Couple Quietly Fixes Up Play Yard."
17. Christopher Klemek, *The Transatlantic Collapse of Urban Renewal* (Chicago: University of Chicago Press, 2011), 187–91.
18. Nicholas Pileggi, "Renaissance of the Upper West Side," *New York Magazine,* June 30, 1969, 29–39.
19. Ira S. Robbins, "Open Space in Public Housing—The New Approach," in *Small Urban Spaces,* ed. Whitney North Seymour Jr. (New York: New York University Press, 1969), 31–32.
20. "Mothers Stage a Happening to Aid 100th Street Playground," *New York Times,* May 6, 1968.
21. Ibid.
22. Marilyn Ryan, in conversation with the author, February 25, 2017.
23. Barbara Campbell, "Two New Play Areas for Central Park Announced by City," *New York Times,* May 16, 1971.
24. "A Children's Play Area with Some New Ideas Is Started in Central Park," *New York Times,* September 29, 1972.
25. Julia Jacquette, *Playground of My Mind* (New York: Prestel, 2017).
26. The museum's expansion is covered in Robert A. M. Stern, *New York 1960: Architecture and Urbanism between the Second World War and the Bicentennial* (New York: Monacelli Press, 1995), 784–97.
27. Letter from Thomas Hoving to August Heckscher, July 18, 1968; Heckscher to Hoving, July 23, 1968; Hoving to Heckscher, July 29, 1968; Heckscher to Hoving, August 5, 1968. Metropolitan Museum of Art File, Municipal Archives.
28. Letter from Jewel H. Bjork to Arthur Rosenblatt, January 17, 1969. Metropolitan Museum of Art File, Municipal Archives.
29. Ada Louise Huxtable, "Metropolitan Museum to Expand in Park and Revamp Collections," *New York Times,* September 29, 1967.
30. Edward C. Burks, "Central Park Building Plans Assailed," *New York Times,* October 11, 1970.
31. Ada Louise Huxtable, "Up in Central Park," *New York Times,* March 19, 1967.
32. Frederick Law Olmsted and Calvert Vaux, "A Review of Recent Changes, and Changes Which Have Been Projected, in the Plans of the Central Park" (1872), in *Forty Years of Landscape Architecture,* ed. Frederick Law Olmsted Jr. and Theodora Kimball (Cambridge, MA: MIT Press, 1973), 248.
33. Stern, *New York 1960,* 771–72.
34. Ada Louise Huxtable, "More on How to Kill a City," *New York Times,* March 21, 1965.
35. "In Central Park—No," *New York Times,* March 17, 1960.
36. Huxtable, "Up in Central Park."
37. The original concept for the playground was even more directly connected to the museum's Egyptian collection, incorporating casts of artifacts. Richard Dattner, in conversation with the author, June 4, 2015.
38. "New Adventure Playground, with Ancient Middle East as Theme, Opens in Central Park," PRCA Press Release, November 30, 1972.

39. Heckscher, *Alive in the City,* 261–63. The commissioner's grandfather, also named August Heckscher, was the original funder of the playground. The Heckscher family's foundation funded the Dattner-designed playground that was destroyed.
40. Edward Ranzal, "Transit Authority Agrees to Modify Central Park Plan," *New York Times,* February 17, 1971.
41. John C. Devlin, "Shouting Mothers Lead Protest against Subway Construction in Central Park," *New York Times,* August 20, 1971.
42. "Central Park Play Site Opens with a Splash," *New York Times,* June 21, 1973.
43. Lisa Hammel, "Playground Is Alive with Running Water and Soaked Children," *New York Times,* June 30, 1973.
44. Ibid.
45. The Louis and Bessie Adler Foundation, a philanthropic organization started by the real estate developer Louis Adler, funded the playground. "Renovated Playground Is Opened in Central Park," October 9, 1970, PRCA Press Release. While it is unclear exactly how this project was initiated, parents in the neighborhood had been petitioning for improvements and the Adler family lived nearby and wanted to invest in the park. Robert Liberman, in conversation, February 6, 2017.
46. Landscape architect Lawrence Halprin explored the connections between design and dance, using the practice of choreography (influenced by his wife, Anna, who was a dancer) to shape his creative process and ultimately "score" a range of interactions with designed spaces. Alison Hirsch, *City Choreographer: Lawrence Halprin in Urban Renewal America* (Minneapolis: University of Minnesota Press, 2014).
47. Alan Kaprow, "Happenings in the New York Scene," in *Essays on the Blurring of Art and Life,* ed. Jeff Kelley (Berkeley: University of California Press, 2003), 17.
48. Quoted in Eva Meyer-Hermann, Andrew Perchuk, and Stephanie Rosenthal, eds., *Alan Kaprow: Art as Life* (Los Angeles: Getty Research Institute, 2008), 68.
49. Weinraub, "A Happening Called Hoving."
50. Bernard Weinraub, "Hoving's Artistic Happening Draws Hundreds to Parks," *New York Times,* May 16, 1966.
51. Ibid.
52. Dan Sullivan, "Avant-Garde Day in the Park Goes On and On," *New York Times,* September 10, 1966.
53. Joan Rothfuss, *Topless Cellist: The Improbable Life of Charlotte Moorman* (Cambridge, MA: MIT Press, 2014), 211.
54. Memo from Reed to Hoving, October 27, 1966. Central Park Files, 1966, Municipal Archives.
55. "The Road to Central Park," *New York Times,* June 30, 1967.
56. M. Paul Friedberg with Ellen Perry Berkeley, *Play and Interplay: A Manifesto for New Design in Urban Recreational Environment* (New York: Macmillan, 1970), 15; Allan Kaprow, *Assemblage, Environments, and Happenings* (New York: H. N. Abrams, 1966), 188.
57. Johan Huizinga, *Homo Ludens: A Study of the Play-Element in Culture* (Boston: Beacon Press, 1966), 5.
58. David M. Grant, "With a Hop, Skip and Jump, Playgrounds Go Modern," *New York Times,* June 17, 1973.
59. This includes playgrounds created for public schools and housing developments and is based on an analysis of Parks Department press releases, the archives of the Park Association, and various newspaper articles.
60. PRCA, *Annual Report of 1967,* n.p.
61. Ada Louis Huxtable, "City Is Building 12 Moveable Playgrounds," *New York Times,* January 28, 1967.
62. M. Paul Friedberg, "Systems for Play," in *Small Urban Spaces.* 116.
63. M. Paul Friedberg, in conversation with the author, January 24, 2017; Friedberg later developed the idea of individual- or community-built playgrounds in a book, which included detailed drawings and instructions for building playgrounds. M. Paul Friedberg, *Handcrafted Playgrounds: Designs You Can Build Yourself* (New York: Random House, 1975).
64. The history of TimberForm is based on conversations with Ken Kirn, who worked with Friedberg on the development of TimberForm and founded Columbia Cascade, January 19, 2016, and with his son Steve Kirn, current sales manager for Columbia Cascade, November 19, 2015. As wood play equipment became more popular, other companies began manufacturing

it, including Big Toys, Natural Structures, and Landscape Structures.

65. Lena Williams, "Children Romp at Dedication of a Playground in Central Park," *New York Times,* November 19, 1976.
66. Tania Long, "Briton Criticizes U.S. Playgrounds," *New York Times,* May 16, 1965.
67. Ada Louis Huxtable, "At Last, a Winner," *New York Times,* May 24, 1966.
68. Playground Corporation of America advertisement, found in *Landscape Architecture* (April 1970): 217.
69. "Play's the Thing," *Architectural Forum,* June 1969; "First of 9 'Instant Playgrounds' Installed in New York City Parks," PRCA Press Release, June 10, 1969. In 2016 Dattner reissued PlayCubes, in collaboration with the play equipment manufacturer Playworld.
70. Lucinda Franks, "An Oasis of Green in Need of Rescue," *New York Times,* March 22, 1974.
71. In October 1972 two exhibitions opened celebrating Olmsted's sesquicentennial, one at the Whitney Museum in New York, the other at the National Gallery in Washington. Elizabeth Barlow wrote the catalog for the Whitney show, *Frederick Law Olmsted's New York* (New York: Praeger, 1972). Other influential books include *Forty Years of Landscape Architecture,* ed. Frederick Law Olmsted Jr. and Theodora Kimball (Cambridge, MA: MIT Press, 1973); and Laura Roper, *FLO: A Biography of Frederick Law Olmsted* (Baltimore: Johns Hopkins University Press, 1973).
72. Albert Fein, *Frederick Law Olmsted and the American Environmental Tradition* (New York: George Braziller, 1972).
73. Heckscher, *Alive in the City,* 162.
74. Robert Makla, Letter to the Editor, *New York Times,* June 17, 1967.
75. "Central Park's Curator Assails Hoving on 'Commercial Invasion,'" *New York Times,* June 27, 1967.
76. "Talk of the Town: Shelter," *New Yorker,* June 13, 1970, 26–27; Ada Louise Huxtable, "Just a Little Love, a Little Care," *New York Times,* December 9, 1973.
77. Lillian Ross, "Talk of the Town: Public Spirited," *New Yorker,* November 25, 1972, 41; "Restored Bow Bridge Reopens to Pedestrians," *New York Times,* September 24, 1974.
78. Adrian and Joseph Bresnan, "Master Plan: A Proposal for a Program of Rehabilitation for Central Park: Design and Construction, 1974–1984" (New York City Department of Parks and Recreation, 1973).
79. Deirdre Carmody, "Quietly, Central Park Advances as Landmark," *New York Times,* March 27, 1974.
80. Allan Siegal, "City's Park System Is Accused of Benign Neglect," *New York Times,* November 8, 1974.
81. Fred Ferretti, "New York Parks Face a Touch-and-Go Summer," *New York Times,* May 26, 1977.
82. E. S. Savas, "A Study of Central Park" (report commissioned by the Central Park Community Fund, 1976); New York Interface Development Project, "An Evaluation of Alternative Governance Proposals for Central Park (report commissioned by the Central Park Community Fund, 1978).

Chapter 4

1. Betsy Barlow, "Expanded Program Statement as of June 3rd Meeting: Design Competition for Playground at 67th Street and Fifth Avenue," undated. Billy Johnson Playground files, Planning, Design, and Construction Files, Central Park Conservancy Archives. (Hereafter CPC Archives.)
2. The conservancy also invited Richard Dattner; Abel, Bainnson and Associates; and Quennell Rothchild and Associates. The judges critiqued Dattner's entry as "far too architectural" (Bronson Binger, assistant commissioner for capital projects, "Schemes, in order of choice," June 22, 1981). Billy Johnson Playground files, CPC Archives.
3. M. Paul Friedberg, Site Plan for Central Park Playground at 67th Street, 1981. Billy Johnson Playground files, CPC Archives.
4. The state of parks in 1980 was captured in a series of three articles called "Paradise Lost? New York City's Parks," in the *New York Times:* Anna Quindlen, "New York City Park System Stands as a Tattered Remnant of Its Past," October 13, 1980; "Parks Plagued by a Shortage of Good Help," October 14, 1980; "City Hoping for Private Operation of Parks," October 15, 1980.

5. Jo Thomas, "On City's Playgrounds, Both Joy and Danger," *New York Times,* August 11, 1986. For a national perspective on playgrounds during this period, see Joe L. Frost, *Play and Playscapes* (Albany, NY: Delmar Publishers, 1992), 205–7.
6. Because of numerous construction problems, the playground took six years to complete, and while some problems were caused by difficulties with a contractor, they were also indicative of the challenge of building custom designs. Letter from M. Paul Friedberg to Betsy Barlow, February 14, 1986. Billy Johnson Playground Files, CPC Archives.
7. Central Park Conservancy and New York City Department of Parks and Recreation, *Rebuilding Central Park: A Management and Restoration Plan* (New York: Central Park Conservancy, 1985).
8. For a history of playground safety, see Henry S. Curtis, *The Practical Conduct of Play* (New York: Macmillan, 1915); Frost, *Play and Playscapes,* 191–208; Donna Thomson, "Organizational Influences on Playground Safety," in *Play It Safe, An Anthology of Playground Safety* (Arlington, VA: National Recreation and Park Association, 1996), 15–28.
9. Susan Solomon has attributed concerns about liability and rising insurance rates as a driving force to changes to American playgrounds during the 1980s. Susan Solomon, *American Playgrounds: Revitalizing Community Space* (Hanover, NH: University Press of New England, 2005), 78–81.
10. Joe Frost, *A History of Children's Play and Play Environments* (New York: Routledge, 2010), 128.
11. Carol Lawson, "Playgrounds Shaped by Today's Urban Concerns," *New York Times,* July 13, 1989; "John Tierney, "Can a Playground Be Too Safe," *New York Times,* July 18, 2011.
12. Douglas Martin, "That Upside-Down High Will Be Only a Memory; Monkey Bars Fall to Safety Pressures," *New York Times,* April 11, 1996.
13. Ibid.
14. Andress Brooks, "How Clean Is Clean Enough," *New York Times,* May 11, 1995.
15. Patricia Leigh Brown, "A Childhood Joy Is Now a Rarity," *New York Times,* May 11, 1995.
16. Although the broken windows theory is now associated with policing, in the 1990s it informed a much broader approach to the urban environment. George L. Kelling and James Q. Wilson, "Broken Windows: The Police and Neighborhood Safety," *Atlantic* (March 1982): 29–38; George L. Kelling. "How New York Became Safe: The Full Story," *City Journal,* Special Issue 2009. http://www.city-journal.org/html/how-new-york-became-safe-full-story-13197.html accessed July 9, 2016.
17. Central Park Conservancy, *Rebuilding Central Park,* 7.
18. For more on thinking about public space at this time, see the Parks Council and the Central Park Conservancy, *Public Space for Public Life: A Plan for the Twenty-first Century* (New York: Parks Council and Central Park Conservancy, December 1993).
19. On the removal of Riis Plaza, see Anne Raver, "When It Goes It's Gone: Manhattan's Vanishing Oases," *New York Times,* December 2, 1999; Paul Bennett, "Social Force: The Urban Optimism of M. Paul Friedberg," in *Preserving Modern Landscape Architecture II: Making Postwar Landscape Visible* (Washington DC: Spacemaker Press, 2004), 35; the New York City Housing Authority does not have any files on the changes to or demolition of Riis Plaza in their archives, nor about the fates of other play spaces they built during the 1960s.
20. Brooke Astor, *Twenty-five Years of Giving in New York* (New York: Vincent Astor Foundation, 1985), 12.
21. Susan Solomon, *American Playgrounds: Revitalizing Community Space* (Hanover, NH: University Press of New England, 2005), 81–88.
22. Howard Chudacoff, *Children at Play: An American History* (New York: New York University Press, 2007), 162–67.
23. Erana Stennett, "Notes from West 67th Street Playground meeting," July 12, 1990. Adventure Playground Files, CPC Archives.
24. "Minutes from the West 67th Street Playground meeting," November 19, 1990. Adventure Playground Files, CPC Archives.
25. Lawson, "Playgrounds Shaped by Today's Urban Concerns."
26. "Playground Fight," *Westside Resident,* August 1–7, 1996.
27. Letter from Richard Dattner to Karen Putnam,

May 7, 1996. Adventure Playground Files, CPC Archives.

28. "Adventure vs. Safety in Playground Renovation Battle," *New York Times,* June 23, 1996; Lincoln Anderson, "Adventure vs. Safety: Visions Clash at 67th Street Playground," *Westsider,* July 4–10, 1996.
29. Toby Axelrod, "Metal to Promote Park Safety, Food to Promote Bike Safety," *New York Observer,* August 19, 1996.
30. Eric Copage, "Neighborhood Report: Upper West Side; A New Version of Adventure for the Kids," *New York Times,* May 30, 1999.
31. Michael Gotkin, "The Politics of Play: The Adventure Playground in Central Park," in Charles Birnbaum, ed., *Preserving Modern Landscape Architecture: Papers from the Wave Hill National Park Service Conference* (Cambridge, MA: Spacemaker Press, 1999): 60–75.
32. A follow-up to this conference was held at Wave Hill and Columbia University in 2002 and conference papers were published in Charles Birnbaum, ed., *Preserving Modern Landscape Architecture II: Making Postwar Landscapes Visible* (Washington, DC: Spacemaker Press, 2004).
33. Charles Birnbaum, "Preserving Contemporary Landscape Architecture: Is Nothing Permanent but Change Itself?" in *Preserving Modern Landscape Architecture,* 6–8.
34. *The Secretary of the Interior's Standards for the Treatment of Historic Properties with Guidelines for the Treatment of Cultural Landscapes* (Washington, DC: US Department of the Interior, 1996), 5.
35. Lisa Crowder, "Playing for Time: Preservation Issues in Contemporary Playground Design," in *Preserving Modern Landscape Architecture,* 56.
36. Ken Smith, "The Challenge of Preserving Lincoln Center for the Performing Arts," in *Preserving Modern Landscape Architecture,* 50.
37. Alison Dalton, "M. Paul Friedberg's Early Playground Design in New York City," in *Preserving Modern Landscape Architecture,* 59.
38. Letter from the Parents Association to Mayor John Lindsay, April 23, 1968. Box 10, Department of Parks files, Vincent Astor Foundation records, Manuscripts and Archives Division, the New York Public Library. (Hereafter VAF records.).
39. Letter from Gloria Johnson (principal) to Linda Gilles (Astor Foundation), November 14, 1975, PS 166 File; Gilles to Johnson, November 25, 1975. Box 10, Department of Parks files, VAF Records.
40. Charles Mee, "Putting the Play in Playgrounds," *New York Times,* November 6, 1966.
41. Charles Birnbaum, ed., *The Secretary of the Interior's Standards for the Treatment of Historic Properties with Guidelines for the Treatments of Cultural Landscapes* (Washington, DC: US Department of the Interior, 1996), 48.
42. Reuben M. Rainey and J. C. Miller, *Modern Public Gardens: Robert Royston and the Suburban Park* (San Francisco: William Stout Publishers).
43. Reed Dillingham and Stephanie Pearson, "Mitchell Park: Rehabilitation of a Modernist Community Play Area," in *Preserve and Play: Preserving Historic Recreation and Entertainment Sites,* ed. Deborah Slaton, Chad Randl, Lauren Van Damme (Washington, DC: National Park Service, 2006), 267–73.
44. Alexandra Lange, "The Great Playscapes," *Why,* October 15, 2014, http://www.hermanmiller.com/why/the-great-playscapes.html (accessed June 22, 2017); Jablonski Berkowitz Conservation, "Conditions Assessment and Repair Recommendations: Noguchi Playscape, Piedmont Park, Atlanta, GA," April 17, 2007.
45. Central Park Conservancy, *Plan for Play* (New York: Central Park Conservancy, 2011).
46. Tim Gill, *No Fear: Growing Up in a Risk-averse Society* (Lisbon: Calouste Gulbenkian Foundation, 2007); Mayor's Office of Long-Term Planning and Sustainability, *PLANYC Progress Report 2010;* Hillary Stout, "Effort to Restore Children's Play Gains Momentum," *New York Times,* January 5, 2011; Richard Louv, *Last Child in the Woods* (Chapel Hill, NC: Algonquin Books, 2005); Stanford Prevention Research Center, Stanford University School of Medicine, *Building "Generation Play": Addressing the Crisis of Inactivity among America's Children* (Palo Alto, CA: Stanford University, February 2007); Dan Jost, "New York Loosens Up," *Landscape Architecture Magazine* 100, no. 11 (November 2010).
47. Frederick Law Olmsted and Calvert Vaux, "Preliminary Report to the Commissioners for Lay-

ing Out a Park in Brooklyn, New York" (1866), in Albert Fein, *Landscape into Cityscape* (New York: Van Nostrand Reinhold, 1981), 98.

48. Robert Smithson, "Frederick Law Olmsted and the Dialectical Landscape," in Jack Flam, ed., *Robert Smithson: The Collected Writings* (Berkeley: University of California Press, 1996), 170.
49. For more detail on the thinking and analysis that went into this process, see Dan Jost, "Resurrecting the 'Adventure-Style' Playground," *Landscape Architecture Magazine* 11, no 3 (March 2010): 44–63.
50. Ibid., 52.
51. Gabriela Burkhalter, *The Playground Project (*Zurich: JRP|Ringier, 2016), 80.
52. Susan Solomon, "Some Thoughts about Preserving Modern Playgrounds," December 16, 2013, http://www.docomomo-us.org/news/some_thoughts_preserving_modern_playgrounds. Accessed April 16, 2017.
53. Paige Johnson, "Thoughts on Playground Preservation, Central Park, New York," October 26, 2012. http://www.play-scapes.com/play-history/mid-century-modern/thoughts-on-playground-preservation-central-park-new-york-city/. Accessed April 16, 2017.
54. Jost, "Resurrecting the 'Adventure-Style' Playground," 54.
55. Gotkin, "Politics of Play," 75.
56. Lady Allen of Hurtwood, *Planning for Play* (London: Thames & Hudson, 1968), 16.
57. For more on ADA and preservation, see Thomas C. Jester and Sharon C. Park, "Preservation Brief: Making Historic Properties Accessible" (Washington, DC: US Department of the Interior, 1993). Designing for children with disabilities was an interest of practitioners during the 1960s and 1970s, including Hurtwood and Dattner. See Hurtwood, *Planning for Play,* 127–37; Richard Dattner, *Design for Play* (New York: Van Nostrand/Reinhold, 1969), 109–17.
58. M. Paul Friedberg with Ellen Perry Berkeley, *Play and Interplay: A Manifesto for New Design in Urban Recreational Environment* (New York: Macmillan, 1970), 44.
59. Ibid., 37.
60. In conversation with Kate Papacosma (Daphne's mother), July 17, 2017.

Selected Bibliography

Aaron, David, with Bonnie P. Winawer. *Childsplay: A Creative Approach to Playscapes for Today's Children*. New York: Harper & Row, 1965.

Alanen, Arnold R., and Robert Z. Melnick, eds. *Preserving Cultural Landscapes in America*. Baltimore: Johns Hopkins University Press, 2000.

Ballon, Hillary, and Kenneth T. Jackson, eds. *Robert Moses and the Modern City: The Transformation of New York*. New York: W. W. Norton & Co., 2007.

Beauregard, Robert A. *Voices of Decline: The Postwar Fate of U.S. Cities*. New York: Routledge, 2003.

Bengtsson, Arvid, ed. *Adventure Playgrounds*. London: Crosby Lockwood Staples, 1973.

Biondo, Brenda. *Once upon a Playground: A Celebration of Classic American Playgrounds, 1920–1975*. Hanover, NH: ForeEdge, 2014.

Birnbaum, Charles, ed. *Preserving Modern Landscape Architecture: Papers from the Wave Hill-National Park Service Conference*. Cambridge, MA: Spacemaker Press, 1999.

——. *Preserving Modern Landscape Architecture II: Making Postwar Landscapes Visible*. Washington, DC: Spacemaker Press, 2004.

——. "Modern Landscape Architecture: Presentation and Preservation," special issue of *Forum Journal* 27, no. 2 (Winter 2013).

Burkhalter, Gabriela. *The Playground Project*. Zurich: JRP/Ringier, 2016.

Bussard, Katherine A., Allison Fisher, and Greg Foster-Rice. *The City Lost and Found: Capturing New York, Chicago, and Los Angeles, 1960–1980*. Princeton, NJ: Princeton University Art Museum, 2014.

Cannato, Vincent. *The Ungovernable City: John Lindsay and His Struggle to Save New York*. New York: Basic Books, 2001.

Central Park Conservancy. *Plan for Play: A Framework for Rebuilding and Managing Central Park Playgrounds*. New York: Central Park Conservancy, 2011.

Central Park Conservancy and New York City Department of Parks and Recreation. *Rebuilding Central Park: A Management and Restoration Plan*. New York: Central Park Conservancy, 1985.

Chudacoff, Howard. *Children at Play: An American History*. New York: New York University Press, 2007.

Cranz, Galen. *The Politics of Park Design: A History of Urban Parks in America*. Cambridge, MA: MIT Press, 1982.

Dattner, Richard. *Design for Play*. New York: Van Nostrand/Reinhold, 1969.

Florence, Jenny. "Pocket Change: New York's Vest-Pock Playgrounds and the Inherited Legacy of Social Reform." MA thesis, Copper-Hewitt, Smithsonian Design Museum/Parsons School of Design, 2012.

Friedberg, M. Paul. *Playgrounds for City Children*. Washington, DC: Association for Childhood Education International, 1969.

Friedberg, M. Paul (with Ellen Perry Berkeley). *Play and Interplay: A Manifesto for New Design in Urban Recreational Environment*. New York: Macmillan, 1970.

——. *Handcrafted Playgrounds: Designs You Can Build Yourself*. New York: Random House, 1975.

——. Oral History Interview. Washington, DC: The Cultural Landscape Foundation, 2009.

Frost, Joe. *Play and Playscapes.* Albany, NY: Delmar Publishers, 1992.

——. *A History of Children's Play and Play Environments.* New York: Routledge, 2010.

Guggenheimer, Elinor. *Planning for Parks and Recreation Needs in Urban Areas.* New York: Twayne Publishers, 1969.

Gotkin, Michael. "The Politics of Play." In *Preserving Modern Landscape Architecture,* ed. Charles Birnbaum, 60–77. New York: Spacemaker Press, 1999.

Gutman, Marta, and Ning de Coninck-Smith. *Designing Modern Childhoods: History, Space, and the Material Culture of Children.* New Brunswick, NJ: Rutgers University Press, 2008.

Harrod, Tanya, Medea Hoch, and Juliet Kinchin. *Century of the Child: Growing by Design 1900–2000.* New York: Museum of Modern Art, 2012.

Heckscher, August. *Alive in the City: A Memoir of an Ex-Commissioner.* New York: Scribner, 1974.

Hurtwood, Lady Allen of. *Planning for Play.* Cambridge, MA: MIT Press, 1968.

Jacobs, Jane. *The Death and Life of Great American Cities.* New York: Random House, 1961.

Jacquette, Julia. *Playground of My Mind.* New York: Prestel, 2017.

Jost, Daniel. "Resurrecting the 'Adventure-Style' Playground." *Landscape Architecture Magazine* 100, no. 3 (March 2010): 44–63.

Kozlovsky, Roy. "Adventure Playgrounds and Postwar Reconstruction." In *Designing Modern Childhoods: History, Space, and the Material Culture of Children*, ed. Marta Gutman and Ning de Coninck-Smith, 171–90. New Brunswick, NJ: Rutgers University Press, 2008.

Larrivee, Shaina D. "Playscapes: Isamu Noguchi's Design for Play." *Public Art Dialogue* 1 (2001): 53–80.

Ledermann, Alfred, and Alfred Trachsel. *Creative Playgrounds and Recreation Centers.* New York: Frederick A. Praeger, 1968.

Longstreth, Richard. *Looking beyond the Icons: Midcentury Architecture, Landscape, and Urbanism.* Charlottesville: University of Virginia Press, 2015.

Mogilevich, Mariana. "Designing the Urban: Space and Politics in Lindsay's New York," PhD diss., Harvard University, 2012.

——. "Arts as Public Policy: Cultural Spaces for Democracy and Growth." In *Summer in the City,* ed. Joseph Viteritti, 195–222. Baltimore: Johns Hopkins University Press, 2014.

Ogata, Amy. *Designing the Creative Child: Playthings and Places in Midcentury America.* Minneapolis: University of Minnesota Press, 2013.

Park Association. *The Citizen and the Parks: Annual Report for 1965.* New York: Park Association, 1966.

——. *The Playground Revolution.* New York: Park Association, 1966.

Roberts, Sam, ed. *America's Mayor: John V. Lindsay and the Reinvention of New York.* New York: Museum of the City of New York and Columbia University Press, 2010.

Rouard, Marguerite, and Jacques Simon. *Children's Play Spaces: From Sandbox to Adventure Playground.* Woodstock, NY: Overlook Press, 1977.

Seymour Jr., Whitney North, ed. *Small Urban Spaces: The Philosophy, Design, Sociology, and Politics of Vest-pocket Parks and Other Small Urban Open Spaces.* New York: New York University Press, 1969.

Solomon, Susan. *American Playgrounds: Revitalizing Community Space.* Hanover, NH: University Press of New England, 2005.

Trainor, James. "Reimagining Recreation," *Cabinet* 45 (Spring 2012), http://www.cabinetmagazine.org/issues/45/trainor.php.

Treib, Marc, ed. *Modern Landscape Architecture: A Critical Review.* Cambridge, MA: MIT Press, 1993.

Walker, Peter, and Melanie Simo, *Invisible Gardens: The Search for Modernism in the American Landscape.* Cambridge, MA: MIT Press, 1996.

Viteritti, Joseph P., ed. *Summer in the City: John Lindsay, New York, and the American Dream.* Baltimore: Johns Hopkins University Press, 2014.

Ward, Colin. *The Child in the City.* New York: Pantheon Books, 1978.

Archives

Administration Files for the Department of Parks. Municipal Archives, New York, NY.

Central Park Conservancy Archives. New York, NY.

Isamu Noguchi Archives. The Isamu Noguchi Foundation and Garden Museum, Long Island City, NY.

Lauder Archives. New York, NY.

Parks Council Records. Avery Architectural & Fine Arts Library, Columbia University, New York, NY.

Vincent Astor Foundation Records. Manuscripts and Archives Division, New York Public Library, New York, NY. New York City Parks Photo Archive, New York, NY.

Image Credits

Figs. 1, 8, 55, 89, 90, 93, 101, 102, 103, 104, 105, 107, 108, 109, 113, 114, 115, 116, 117, 118, 119, 120, 121, 123, 124, 126, 127, 128, 129, 131, 132, 133, 134, 135, 136, 137, 138: Courtesy of the Central Park Conservancy

Figs. 2, 30, 38, 39, 67, 68, 69, 70, 71, 72, 73, 74, 76, 88, 94: Courtesy of Richard Dattner

Figs. 3, 7, 22, 24, 26, 27, 32, 33, 35, 43, 44, 48, 52, 53, 54, 56, 57, 58, 66, 75, 77, 78, 79, 80, 81, 82, 83, 84, 92, 106, 122, 139, 140: New York City Parks Photo Archive

Figs. 4, 11, 10, 13: The Miriam and Ira D. Wallach Division of Art, Prints and Photographs: Photography Collection, the New York Public Library

Fig. 5: Courtesy of the National Park Service, Frederick Law Olmsted National Historic Site

Figs. 6, 14, 17, 19, 21: Library of Congress Prints and Photographs Division

Fig. 9: Milstein Division, New York Public Library

Figs. 45, 46, 47: Manuscripts and Archives Division, the New York Public Library, Astor, Lenox and Tilden Foundations. Photos by David Hirsch.

Figs. 12, 20: Private Collection

Fig. 15: Jacob A. (Jacob August) Riis (1849–1914)/Museum of the City of New York. 90.13.2.296

Figs. 16, 18: Courtesy of the Frances Loeb Library, Harvard Graduate School of Design

Fig. 23: Arnold Eagle for Federal Art Project/Museum of the City of New York. 43.131.11.410

Figs. 25, 31, 91, 100: New York City Parks Map File

Fig. 28: Photo by Tom Baffer/New York Daily News Archive via Getty Images

Fig. 29: Courtesy of NYC Municipal Archives

Figs. 34, 49, 50, 95, 96, 97, 99: Copyright Ruth Orkin

Figs. 36, 37: Copyright Museum of London

Fig. 40: The Isamu Noguchi Foundation and Garden Museum, New York. © The Isamu Noguchi Foundation and Garden Museum, New York / ARS. Photographer unknown.

Fig. 41: The Isamu Noguchi Foundation and Garden Museum, New York. ©The Isamu Noguchi Foundation and Garden Museum, New York / ARS. Photo by Charles Uht.

Fig. 42: The Isamu Noguchi Foundation and Garden Museum, New York. ©The Isamu Noguchi Foundation and Garden Museum, New York / ARS. Photo by Kevin Noble.

Fig. 51: Photo by Barton Silverman/New York Times/Redux

Fig. 59: New York City Housing Authority

Figs. 60, 62, 63, 64, 125: Courtesy of William Jacquette

Figs. 61, 130: Courtesy of Marilyn Ryan

Figs. 65: Courtesy of MTA Bridges and Tunnels Special Archive

Fig. 85: George McCue Photograph Collection, 718.231, the State Historical Society of Missouri, Photograph Collection.

Fig. 86, 87: Courtesy of Columbia Cascade. Photos by Ron Green.

Fig. 98: Photo by Jack Manning/New York Times/Redux

Fig. 110: Courtesy of RHAA Landscape Architects

Fig. 111: Courtesy of the Cultural Landscape Foundation. Photo by Charles Birnbaum.

Figs. 112, 139, 141: Courtesy of the author